Engaging Diverse Learners

Engaging Diverse Learners

Teaching Strategies for Academic Librarians

Mark Aaron Polger and Scott Sheidlower

An Imprint of ABC-CLIO, LLC

Santa Barbara, California • Denver, Colorado

Library of Congress Cataloging-in-Publication Data

Names: Polger, Mark Aaron, author. | Sheidlower, Scott, author.
Title: Engaging diverse learners : teaching strategies for academic librarians /
    Mark Aaron Polger and Scott Sheidlower.
Description: Santa Barbara, California : Libraries Unlimited, an imprint of ABC-CLIO,
    LLC, [2017] | Includes bibliographical references and index.
Identifiers: LCCN 2016049264 (print) | LCCN 2017000746 (ebook) |
    ISBN 9781440838507 (paperback : acid-free paper) | ISBN 9781440838514 (ebook)
Subjects: LCSH: Information literacy—Study and teaching (Higher) | Library
    orientation for college students. | Instruction librarians. | Academic librarians. |
    Engagement (Philosophy) | Motivation in education. | Effective teaching. |
    Information literacy—Study and teaching (Higher)—United States—Case studies.
Classification: LCC ZA3075 .P65 2017 (print) | LCC ZA3075 (ebook) |
    DDC 025.5/677—dc23
LC record available at https://lccn.loc.gov/2016049264

ISBN: 978-1-4408-3850-7
EISBN: 978-1-4408-3851-4

21 20 19 18 17   1 2 3 4 5

This book is also available as an eBook.

Libraries Unlimited
An Imprint of ABC-CLIO, LLC

ABC-CLIO, LLC
130 Cremona Drive, P.O. Box 1911
Santa Barbara, California 93116–1911
www.abc-clio.com

This book is printed on acid-free paper ∞

Manufactured in the United States of America

This book is dedicated to Mark's late spouse Paulo J. S. Pereira
(January 15, 1972–December 4, 2012)

Thank you Paulo for being in my life. I'm so happy we met that summer in August of 2000 right after I graduated from library school. The years that followed were quite the adventure. Thanks for 12 years of friendship and the romantic roller-coaster journey that followed. In sickness and in health, you were always a supportive friend and later, spouse. You always supported my career, my teaching, my desire to help people. You always relied on me for doing credible research for you. Thank you for respecting the craft of librarianship, a profession that so many disrespect, dismiss, and disregard. It was bittersweet when the 2014 ALA Annual Conference was held in Las Vegas, a city that you loved so much. When I attended the conference and visited the city for the first time, I felt your presence everywhere. It was special.

Thank you for taking care of me, even when you became terminally ill. I am grateful for your love, support, crass humor, and political incorrectness. I enjoyed our engaging discussions and debates we have had over the years. There is so much of you that I have carried on in my life (except the sarcasm and cigarettes). Your workaholic personality, your determination to succeed and excel in life, and your desire to please people, lives on in me. I am thankful for our years together. Wherever you are, you are terribly missed.

Je t'aime.

Contents

Acknowledgments

Unlike academia, we are inspired by the schoolteachers in the community who are actually trained on how to teach. Whether it is primary or secondary education, we base much of our pedagogical practices on how they teach in their classrooms.

Teaching is both exhausting and energizing at the same time. When both authors graduated library school in 2000, we were never taught how to teach. In fact, we never expected to teach any classes when we graduated. When we became librarians, we expected most of our time being on the reference desk assisting students with their information needs. References services, a common function of all librarians, has vastly changed over the last twenty years. Most of our daily responsibilities involves classroom teaching. Many of our survey respondents feel that teaching is a performance. Learning how to teach effectively requires continuous practice, dedication, and trial and error, just like a theatrical performance.

Mark Aaron Polger would like to thank:

- My friend and coauthor Scott Sheidlower for this collaboration. It was fun meeting at each other's apartments, brainstorming, arguing, researching, reading, learning, writing, enjoying bagels and tofu cream cheese, and surrounding our world with cats. It has been a long journey and I am happy the stress is over. Cheers to our first major collaboration!

- My parents Leona and David Polger, who have been my allies throughout my life. Thanks for always stepping in, during the good and the bad. They have consistently been supportive forces who have unfailingly pushed me to pursue both my personal and professional interests. I am so lucky to have such loving parents who have been wonderful role models in my life.

- My sister Stephanie Polger and brother-in-law David Handelman.

- My colleagues at the CSI Library: Professor Amy F. Stempler who has always supported me in my teaching and Associate Dean Dr. Wilma P.L. Jones for giving the "ok" for a credit bearing Information Literacy course after years of convincing, and Professor Allen Natowitz, for being the best mentor during my years leading up to tenure.

- My colleagues at ASA College, where I have enjoyed teaching since 2011: Brook Stowe, Bridget Udeh, Julia Agoglia, Joy Dunkley, Lorna Kilkenny, Toni Ann Kaminski, Albert Tablante, Michael Kahn, Wendy Roque, Eileen Ressler, Pamela Pollack, Nathan Atwood, Denise Dubron, Anne Swain, Annie Mak, and C. Yvonne Palmer.

- The Executive Board of the New York State Teachers of English to Speakers of Other Languages (NYS TESOL). It has been a great experience being involved with this wonderful organization these past five years.

- The Executive Board of the Association of College and Research Libraries, Greater Metropolitan New York City area (ACRL/NY).

- My professional mentor and friend Janice Rosen, Archives Director of the Canadian Jewish Archives in Montreal, Canada (formerly the Canadian Jewish Congress National Archives), where I worked as an archives assistant from 1993 to 1999.

- My library marketing mentor Kathy Dempsey. You are a great colleague to work with. You continue to inspire me with your passion for library marketing!

- The planning committee of the Library Marketing and Communications Conference (LMCC); I am honored to be part of this conference planning team.

- My colleagues at ACRL National's Library Marketing and Outreach Interest Group: Virginia Alexander Cononie, Amy Wainwright, Christopher Davidson, and Bonnie Cohen Lafazan.

- The American Library Association's LLAMA PRMS PR Xchange Team: Fred Reuland, Kerry Ward, Rebecca Metzger, Joyce Garczynski, Holly Flynn, Alison Armstrong, and many others.

- My previous cochairs of the Annual LLAMA PRMS PR Xchange Awards Competition: Laura Tomcik, Scott Sheidlower, and Karen Okamoto.

- My cochairs Robin O'Hanlon and Maria Deptula of the Greater NYC ACRL Library Marketing and Outreach Interest Group.

- My cochair Carl Andrews of the New York Metropolitan Library Council (METRO) Outreach and Advocacy Special Interest Group.

- My cochair Carlos Arguelles of the Library Marketing and Outreach Roundtable Discussion Group of the Library Association of the City University of New York (LACUNY).

- Tina Paglia for encouraging me to pursue teaching way back in 2004.

- Ann Hersch and Carlisle Kemp-Jackson, former LIT coordinators at Seneca College in Toronto, Canada. I was referred by Tina Paglia at Vaughan Public Libraries in late 2004 and I was asked to come in for an informal interview in late 2004. Becoming a college instructor was a turning point in my life. I must thank Ann and Carlisle for believing in me. I was fortunate to teach four courses in Seneca College's Library and Information Technician Program from 2005 to 2008. During this time, I fell in love with teaching and this passion continued into my eventual move to New York City in 2008.

- Dolores Harms Penner at Mohawk College's Library and Information Technician Program in Hamilton, Ontario, Canada.

- My dear friends, family, and colleagues in New York City, Toronto, Montreal, and London (Canada): Wendy Furtenbacher and Don Madonna, Vivian Bejerman and Adam Leiner, Kinga Breining and Peter Kiss, Elizabeth (Lisa) Palov, Mason Cooper and Julie Miller, Maxine and Tony D'Alfonso, Beth Hurley and Ryan Hurley, Aaron Boros and Daniel Malen, Marlin Roy, Dimitry Epelbaum and Andrew Grudek, Cindy Goldberg, Pamela Feigen and Sarah Smith, Sandi Burgess, Tammy Moorse, Jennifer Dunne, Faline Bobier, Susanne Marcus Solomkin, David Solomkin, and Jennie Solomkin, Shari and Raffi Kopla, Lynn Marcus, David and Anita Marcus, Linda and Shlomo Oren, Susan Yegendorf, Barbara and Simon Abecassis, David Abecassis, Robert (Bob) Zavitz, Jana Leslie Stuart, Christine Oakes, Abdul Pullattayil, Leona Dove, Carmen Alcalde, Christy Sich and Dan Sich, Justine Apple and Ronni Teitelbaum, Karen Okamoto and Antonio (Tony) D'Souza, Alice Lam, Joel Moses, Joel Sacks and Walter Apai, Heidi Furtenbacher, Wendy Cramer, Michael Barcham, Laura Solomon, Madelena Montiel, Stefanie Havelka, Joan Petit, Tom Klem and Warren Friedman, Pamela Pollack, Suha Kudsieh, Zamin Kanji and Asim Ashraf, Naomi Gold, Merline Xavier, Catherine Healey, Rose Ann Delli Paoli, Pamela Jones, and Kelly Hamilton.

- My dear friend Dr. Jay Bernstein (Kingsborough Community College, City University of New York), who passed away this summer (2016). Jay was deeply engaged in service and scholarship and I admired his dedication to librarianship. Unfortunately, he was the victim of workplace bullying and his body and spirit gave up. I'm sorry he was not able to see the book come to fruition. His death has been a jolt for much of the CUNY library community.

- My favorite teachers in university: Heather Angela Ford-Rosenthal (Concordia University) and Dr. Alicja Muszynski (University of Waterloo).

- My former students from Seneca College whom I still keep in touch with over 12 years later: Martha Jennings, Elise Brais, Jodi Leigh Thomas, Patricia Talarowski, and Kathryn Cipp Quitasol.

- The American Library Association for accrediting my master of library science degree so I can work in the United States.

- The College of Staten Island, City University of New York, for sponsoring me for an H-1B work visa, which lead to a green card, and later, U.S. citizenship.

- My cats Oliver Bartholomew, Grace Elizabeth, Sofia Simone, and my dearly departed Hope Emma.

- My better half Keith Saks, for your support, your million-dollar smile, your politically incorrect sarcasm, your superb cooking, your quintessential Brooklyn aura, your daily weather reports, the ridiculous nicknames you give me, and your overall great sense of humor. Thanks for taking care of Oliver and me during our most difficult times.

- Last but not least, the many teaching librarians who responded to our questionnaire, and to those who agreed to be interviewed for the book.

Scott Sheidlower would like to thank:

- My good friend Mark Aaron Polger for being a great writing partner. I would also like to thank my colleagues at York College in Jamaica, Queens, and throughout the City University of New York system for their support during the writing of this book.

- The Professional Staff Congress, especially Sam Rasiotis, the organizer for my chapter at York College, our union for faculty, Higher Education Officers (HEOs), and College Laboratory Technicians (CLTs) for all of their inspiration.

- Grace Avila, Professor Daniel Cleary, Professor John Drobnicki, Travis Hilton, Professor Njoki Kinyatti, Kenneth Krepp, Professor Christina Miller, Professor Di Su, Professor Todd Simpson, and Professor Holly Skir.

- My friends and family who helped me write through their support: Mrs. Ruth Sheidlower, my mom; David Sheidlower, my brother; both Isaac Sheidlower and Nathaniel Sheidlower, my two nephews. Finally, I would like to thank the clergy and congregation of the Stephen Wise Free Synagogue, all of whom were very supportive. Anyone I forgot to include, please forgive me and know that when you read this book, you helped to bring it to fruition.

- The doormen in Mark's building who no longer look at me suspiciously when I come to work with Mark on a weekly basis.

- Last but certainly not least, I would like to thank Gracie and Sofia, my two adorable foster pussycats.

Both Mark Aaron Polger and Scott Sheidlower would like to thank:

- Libraries Unlimited/ABC-CLIO for believing in this project and the hard work of both of our editors, Lise Dyckman and Sharon Coatney.

- Finally, we would like to thank the librarians who shared their teaching strategies with us.

We appreciate you sharing your expertise and creativity with us. These librarians' names are listed below in alphabetical order.

Dr. Shelley Blundell
Professor Alexandra Deluise
Professor John Drobnicki
Professor Lisa Ellis
Nancy Falciani-White
Dr. Naomi Gold
Kelly Hamilton
Michael Kahn
Toni Ann Kaminski
Robin O'Hanlon
Professor Karen Okamoto
Professor Steven Ovadia
Daniel Payne
Pamela Pollack
Elaine Provenzano
Professor Mariana Regalado
Dan Sich
Dr. Maura Smale
Eamon Tewell
Rachel Wexelbaum (chapter 3)
Linda P. Yau

A Short Introduction: "OMG," Another Library Lesson!

I've heard this librarian say the same thing more than 100 times.
> —An irritated student in a library class

Have you ever entered a classroom in your library building or in any other building on your campus prepared to teach an information literacy lesson (or any lesson related to the library for that matter) and seen a sea of blank faces? Once you have started teaching, have the iPhones, iPads, and so on popped out? In that case, have you enjoyed the sound of your own voice? By the end of the lesson do you think that the students have either heard or paid attention to most of the things you have said? Will they use what you have taught them during that lesson the following week or during the rest of the semester? Or do you wish you could have been doing something else more productive? How do you get those students whose attention is wandering to both pay attention and remember?

What Is This Book About?

As the title of this volume suggests, this book explores how librarians can employ different teaching strategies to best engage different types of learners in the library classroom. bell hooks writes that teaching is a performative act (hooks, 1994) and engagement represents the commitment to be involved or participate in this performance. This book contains groups of techniques, various theories, and multiple ideas to make your teaching more engaging in the library classroom. Although this book was conceived as being mainly practical in nature, it also includes a research study involving an anonymous questionnaire (that was taken and submitted by 900 respondents) administered by the authors, in addition to interviews from over 20 teaching librarians. The authors hope to offer both practical and theoretical perspectives about the concept of engagement, how to engage, how to assess engagement, and a plethora of teaching strategies that may promote engagement.

In her writing, Stebbins (2015, p. xviii) defines the "drool bucket phenomenon." She defines "drool bucket" as an example of Air Force slang that describes the overload of information that Air Force pilots can experience when dealing with the huge amount of data that they receive from their instruments. This leads to the pilots becoming "lost and staring unblinkingly into massive data systems" (Stebbins, 2015, p. xviii). Obviously, any student who is dealing with the "drool bucket phenomenon" is not, at that moment, engaged. The purpose of this book is to help the librarian overcome this phenomenon and engage the students in the class.

Each of the book's chapters explores the process of understanding the diversity of our learners, and establishing different strategies and techniques to successfully engage them in the librarian's lesson. Different learners acquire knowledge differently, and different librarians teach differently. Since teaching and learning are meant to be an exchange, engagement may represent the perfect recipe of the combination of teaching and learning. Engagement is a two-way street. If students are engaged, then the instructor is generally engaged as well. If the instructor is passionate about the lesson, then the students might have a higher chance of being engaged. The reverse is also true. If the instructor is not engaged and is bored, then the students may be able to read the signs of a disengaged instructor and they will be uninvolved. If the students are bored, then the instructor could feel an equal lack of enthusiasm or of motivation to do his or her best, and this will be reflected in his or her teaching and hence in the students' learning.

Navigating the Book

Each of the chapters deals with one of three things: (1) theories about education and engagement, (2) practical teaching techniques to engage diverse learners, or (3) the research questionnaire we administered and analyzed.

Chapter 1 concerns itself with defining engagement and with theories of educational engagement. This first chapter also delves into our questionnaire ($N = 900$), administered in December 2014, in which we explored different conceptualizations of the meaning of engagement. The questionnaire further focused on how academic librarians engage their students, how they assess that engagement, and what external factors may affect students' level of engagement. The questionnaire data is discussed in Chapters 1 and 4. The appendix includes the full questionnaire.

Chapter 2 focuses on the question of "Who are our learners?" It looks closely at the generations of learners we may encounter in the classroom, for example, baby boomers and millennials.

Chapter 3 studies various types of learners from a viewpoint of diversity and multiculturalism. An illustration of this is how to teach different groups such as teaching the disabled versus teaching students of color.

Chapter 4 is the largest chapter and covers various teaching techniques the reader may use to keep students engaged. In addition to culling library literature and the authors' professional experience as teachers, this chapter also includes in-depth qualitative data from interviews from over 20 instruction librarians from different academic institutions in the United States and Canada. This chapter also examines some of the practical data culled from our questionnaire on student engagement.

Chapter 5 analyzes the various learning spaces that exist outside of the classroom, such as the reference desk as well as online environments such as learning management systems, for example, Blackboard, Moodle, and massive open online courses (MOOCs).

Chapter 6 delves into understanding student disengagement, the possible factors that make engagement more challenging, and how librarians should not see disengagement as failure on their own part to teach, but as an opportunity to understand that student engagement depends on many external factors, some of which are out of our own control.

Chapter 7 focuses on the various ways we can incorporate engagement as part of the library's strategic marketing plan. Some examples of this are how to brand your teaching style, how to engage students during new student orientation presentations and library tours, and how to engage students in your outreach endeavors.

Each of the chapters starts with an actual quote from an authority on the literature on student engagement, or an actual response from our questionnaire that we used to complement this book. There is no "right" formula to successfully engage students when teaching. This book does not serve as a "how to teach" but it offers practical teaching strategies specifically for the library classroom.

CHAPTER ONE

Defining Engagement

Student engagement is the product of motivation and active learning.
—Elizabeth Barkley, 2010

This book's theme concerns how we as academic librarians engage students in the classroom. In order to place this idea into a more focused context, we are concentrating on the library classroom. Throughout this book, we also want to be open and inclusive of what engagement means. Engagement depends on many factors. Obviously, those involved the librarian and his/her students and the contexts in which these people are being engaged, for example, how hungry or how tired the student is; most of these contexts are outside of the librarian's control. There are many levels of engagement, and this book aims to focus on strategies used to make meaningful connections with our students. In education, engagement can be defined not only as connections but also as involvement. An example of this is found in the following sentence from Denda, "As our world becomes more and more visually oriented, visual literacy is an arena of fruitful engagement for academic librarians and worthy of critical attention" (2015, p. 300).

The authors define student engagement as the ability to teach students on any level such that they are able to connect with the content being taught. Student engagement involves a set of behaviors, practices, or techniques used to connect the academic librarians with their students. Student engagement also relates to a successful partnership in teaching and learning between the instructor and the learner.

One such example of how this works is more fully described in Chapter 3, where there is an extended discussion of queer students. This is studied here in spite of the fact that "There is currently no evidence to support the idea that LGBT[QI] students learn differently from their heterosexual peers" (Renn, 1998, p. 233). The key point in this book is about how to engage students however you teach them, not how to go about teaching them. We do not have a separate section on how gender issues affect engagement and learning.

Including feminist theory and bringing in the concept of intersectionality or "the interaction between gender, race, and other categories of difference in individual lives, social practices, institutional arrangements, and cultural ideologies and the outcomes of these interactions in terms of power" (Davis, 2008, p. 68) would just complicate this book more than was necessary.

The National Survey of Student Engagement (NSSE) is based on the Seven Principles of Good Practice in Undergraduate Education, which states "that level of academic challenge, time on task, and participating in other educationally purposeful activities directly influence the quality of student learning and their overall educational experience" (Kuh, 2001, p. 12). The principles were developed in 1986 at a conference held at the Wingspread Conference Center in Racine, Wisconsin, which was called in order to distill research findings on teaching and learning in higher education.

Chickering and Garrison (1987) discuss student engagement principles as follows. They:

- encourage contact between students and faculty,
- develop reciprocity and cooperation among students,
- encourage active learning,
- give prompt feedback,
- emphasize time on task,
- communicate high expectations, and
- respect diverse talents and ways of learning.

Similar to a romantic engagement, where two people proclaim their love for each other and their engagement relates to a commitment to being together, the authors believe that student engagement relates to a type of commitment as well. In an ideal world, engagement in the classroom relates to teachers committing to teach and students committing to learn.

It might resemble the careful recipe of the interactions between student, faculty member, class content, and the librarian's teaching. Just like a cake recipe, engagement can be affected by a variety of external factors outside of the academic librarian's purview or control.

Gibson (2006) quotes Stephen Bowen, a Senior Fellow of the Association of American Colleges and Universities, as stating that there are four types of student engagement: "student engagement with the learning process; student engagement with the object of study; student engagement with contexts; and student engagement with the human condition" (p. vii).

Engagement can also be about the lasting effects that students continue to have after the class. If a student feels inspired to learn and his or her experiences of the class were memorable, then this is another level of engagement. At its most basic, one wants to connect to students' mind and leave them with at least one mental takeaway. As any librarian who has ever taught in a classroom knows, this is a lot easier to say than to do. As children's literature shows, a student in the United States often has his or her first library lesson in elementary school (for example, Thaler, 2008), yet by the time students get to college, the library is a confusing place to many of them. What has happened to them?

College students, especially millennials, feel more independent and capable of doing their own research because of the World Wide Web. Unfortunately, they do not feel the need to consult the librarian's expertise, and this may result in not gaining access to the highest quality information sources. Classroom faculty have the same or similar problems. As Hagopian observes:

> How bad has it gotten in your class? Students eating steaming plate lunches, kissing passionately, conducting loud phone conversations, playing video poker? Students refusing to complete group work, ignoring demands to appear for an office session, or using obscenities in e-mails and on evaluations? How about claiming that an undiagnosed learning disability made it impossible for the student ever to attend the class for which she is enrolled? Asking to be excused from class to "barbecue chicken at the go-kart track for a radio station" where the student interned last summer? The term we use to describe these student behaviors is entitlement. (2013, p. 7)

The instructional librarian's role is to organize information and to be able to teach others how to effectively access this information. During the teaching process, we attempt to accomplish at least three objectives:

- We teach skills that will apply to all academic disciplines (and life skills).
- We promote our services and resources in our classes while we teach.
- The unspoken learning objective is to keep the students' attention (Vossler & Sheidlower, 2011).

Keeping students' attention is only a small part of the student engagement equation. Librarians connect differently with different patrons/learners according to the various needs, which are often defined by that patron's identity. This book will address different types of patrons/learners whom a modern academic librarian can expect to interact with and give them tools to keep these students engaged.

Defining Engagement

The word "engagement" is multifaceted. It can mean many things from two armies opposing each other on the battlefield, as in country A engaged with country B in the battle that won the war, to something much more tender as in *he got down on one knee before his lover and proposed, and seconds later, they were engaged.*

One thing that is true no matter how the reader's defines engagement is that engagement is a connection within a specific context. An illustration of this taken from the previous examples would be if the president of country A got down on his knees and proposes marriage to the president of country B and then sent in his troops to invade country B. When asked why he did that, he answers that by proposing marriage he had declared war. Obviously, while married couples may fight, a marriage proposal by itself is not a declaration of war.

While all of the above may be true, in this book, "engagement" will be used to reflect the outcome of the various strategies we will discuss that keep any group of students interested and involved in whatever the academic librarian is teaching.

Even though the focus of this volume is related to engagement as it relates to teaching, the authors recognize that it is not solely limited to that function in the library. Librarians and libraries attempt to engage their users through marketing, programming, signage, advocacy, fund-raising, the decor and design of their space, and so on.

Libraries may partner with other academic units on campus to engage users to help in retention and enrollment and assist in alumni relations (Bell, 2008; Haddow & Joseph, 2010).

As George D. Kuh and Robert M. Gonyea (2003, p. 259) noted, ". . . more engaged students are in these and other educationally purposeful activities, the more likely they are to engage fully in productive activities after college, including civic participation and so on."

Student Engagement Is a Two-Way Street

This book further concentrates on techniques to engage the student. It is not a theoretical treatise. These techniques could possibly work regardless of whether you are teaching to the Association of College and Research Libraries' (ACRL) Information Literacy Competency Standards for Higher Education (American Library Association, Association of College and Research Libraries, 2000) or to the ACRL's new Framework for Information Literacy for Higher Education (American Library Association, Association of College and Research Libraries, 2015) or to some other locally created or nationally used or internationally generated document. It does not matter which technique you use or how you use it; as the heading states, student engagement is a two-way street. No matter what the librarian does, if the students are more interested in their job, their Internal Revenue Service (IRS) bill, what's for dinner, and so on, they will not get anything out of the lesson.

The literature on engagement focuses mostly on student library usage (Smallwood, 2012; Snavely, 2012) or on staff retention (VanDuinkerken & Mosley, 2011). Snavely (2012) mostly focuses on student engagement (in the library) but also focuses on the bigger picture, increased student use of the library. Some of the literature focuses on targeting specific users, for example, international students (Amsberry, 2012) or undergraduate students (Snavely, 2012; Daly, 2012); other library literature deals with collaboration (Girven, 2012). White (2012) discusses how the development of a marketing plan (written by students) can help increase library use. Scull (2014) focuses on collaboration with students who create LibGuides (as a research assignment) for the library. Kuh and Gonyea (2003) analyzed two student samples from the College Student Experience Questionnaire (CSEQ). Their first sample analyzed 300,000 students from the second, third, and fourth editions of the CSEQ from 1984 to 2002. Their second sample was a subsample of the first sample and comprised 80,000 full-time students only from the fourth edition of the CSEQ from 1998 to 2002. They found that student engagement was operationalized as communicating with faculty, their peers, and their overall satisfaction in college. Kuh and Gonyea (2003) also argue that the more engaged students are, the more connected they are to their community after college.

This book diverges from a norm as seen in Snavely (2012). It has been written to give the librarian a variety of teaching techniques to help students learn information literacy concepts. As librarians, we must engage the students' attention and imagination so that they remember what we teach them of information literacy because we cannot trust teaching faculty to make it as important as we believe it is. Flaspohler (2012, p. 75) notes in her review of Claire McGuiness's 2006 longitudinal study of Irish teaching faculty that "most teaching faculty report subscribing to one or more of the following theories":

1. *The Heads in the Sand Theory*: There continue to be teaching faculty who believe that they are *already* teaching information literacy competencies well enough, thank you very much. McGuiness reports that among the faculty she surveyed, "there was a tacit assumption . . . that students would somehow absorb and develop the requisite knowledge and skills through the very process of preparing a written piece of coursework" (McGuiness, 2006, p. 577). While these teaching faculty do not explicitly articulate information literacy outcomes for their courses or show their students how to find academic research with any intentionality, they nevertheless believe that they are currently doing a good enough job at getting students into the library.

2. *The Sink or Swim Theory*: McGuiness found that some teaching faculty believe that whether or not a student becomes information literate "depends almost entirely on personal interest, individual motivation and innate ability, rather than on the quality and format of available instructional opportunities" (McGuiness, 2006, p. 577). These faculty members may rely on antiquated memories of their own formative library experiences relying on the assumption that since they were able to figure library research out on their own, today's millennial students will certainly be able to do the same.

3. *The Osmosis Theory*: Finally, McGuinness identified teaching faculty who seem to feel that having a formal structure for promoting information literacy is unnecessary. Rather, these faculty members see information literacy competency as a "natural, almost intuitive process, whereby students will somehow work it out though encountering and resolving information problems throughout the course of their education" (McGuiness, 2006, p. 578). These faculty members are confident that their students attain information literacy proficiency, and yet, these professors are usually, "unable to explain the mechanism by which it occurs" (McGuiness, 2006, p. 578).

Another way for the class to be more engaged might be termed an *Authenticity Theory*. If librarians are being more than their authentic self, then they will be more engaged in their scholarship, and hence their job. An example of this is found in McNaron (1997) who did a survey that included a lesbian librarian [discussing coming out of the closet professionally] with 24 years' experience at a large state university [who] said this:

"I feel more *alive* than I've ever been because I am being *me*. I have compiled a 100+ page bibliography of lesbian/gay material in the library system for the campus community, am writing an article on [a new museum], am the chair of [two gay/lesbian caucus committees of her professional association], taught a [women's studies] course (spring of 1994)."—"Out of the Closet and Into View, Art History from the Gay/Lesbian Perspective" (McNaron, p. 99)

McGuinness (2012) includes two additional pedagogically related findings in her article. First, she documents teaching faculty who believe that most students "learn how to be information literate through working with their fellow students and turning to their peers," (McGuiness, 2006, p. 579). Second, she identifies faculty who believe that information literacy competency seems to naturally evolve as a result " of being confronted with an unfamiliar situation or a seemingly intractable information problem" (McGuiness, 2006, p. 579).

For these last faculty members, the often haphazard technique of painstakingly "working out how to achieve a satisfactory solution or find an appropriate answer to a question" is the main method responsible for imparting information literacy competencies among their students (McGuiness, 2006, p. 579).

The authors recognize that teaching information literacy is similar to teaching any other college-level skill. It can be shown to the students but the teacher must help them learn.

The rest of this book is concerned with techniques and theories to help the students learn. While this volume does not specifically focus on the theory of critical pedagogy (see Freire discussed in the next section), education can be oppressive and teaching must be carefully used so it does not repress students, especially minority students (Kincheloe, 2004). Nonetheless, many of the techniques in this book, especially those in Chapter 2, deal with specific groups such as LGBTQI students, by offering techniques that deal with diverse learners.

Three Educational Theorists of the Mid-Twentieth Century and Engagement

In the middle of the twentieth century, teaching was defined by three educational theorists: American educators Benjamin Bloom (1913–1999) and Howard Gardner (1943–) and Brazilian educator Paulo Freire (1921–1997). Both Bloom and Freire seem to have been concerned with how teachers could best teach students but Gardner was most interested in how students learn. Bloom created a theory called "Bloom's Taxonomy of learning objectives" in 1956. It is better known as "Bloom's Taxonomy." This taxonomy aimed to look at student's cognition and to help students reach "the realization of the educational goals" (Eisner, 2000, p. 391) of the curriculum being studied. It is divided into six levels (Bloom, 1956).

According to Benjamin Bloom (1956), and his colleagues, there are six levels of cognition:

1. Knowledge: rote memorization, recognition, or recall of facts
2. Comprehension: understanding what the facts mean
3. Application: correct use of the facts, rules, or ideas
4. Analysis: breaking down information into component parts
5. Synthesis: combination of facts, ideas, or information to make a new whole
6. Evaluation: judging or forming an opinion about the information or situation

Bloom's basic assumption is that if you teach well, students will be interested and pay attention. He was more interested in how teachers teach than in how students do their job of listening and learning. The authors of this book are certain that the readers have planned and taught a very good library lesson, and in spite of this they have had students ignore them.

Freire was a Brazilian Christian educator who worked to educate for liberation (Mithra, 2014). He used engagement in a "cultural and political context [in connection with] the left-wing Christian [theoreticians of the 1960s]" (Andreola, 2012, p. 122). In Freire's book *Education and Change* (Andreola, 2012, p. 123), engagement is defined as a form of commitment: "Commitment, which is characteristic of human existence, only exists in engagement with reality, whose 'waters' 'wet' or rather drench men who are truly committed. Only in this way is there true commitment." To Freire, "engagement always means, above all, ethical and political commitment. It is only so that a life and work take on the dimensions of prophetic testimony, denunciation and announcement, which means, in addition, an openness in the perspective of utopia, in the horizon of hope, dimensions without which the action would entirely lack meaning" (Andreola, 2012, p. 123).

When we write about engagement in this book, we are not writing about Freire's philosophical ideas, which were there to show the teacher how to teach and approach their subject matter. Rather we are looking at more student-centered learning. How can a teacher get the student to be more involved in the lesson(s)? For this, Gardner's work is more relevant.

In 1983, Howard Gardner, a Harvard psychologist, wrote *Frames of Mind* (Gardner, 1998). His theory, of multiple intelligences, is more connected to this book. It is based upon the idea that different people learn in different ways, and if you want students to learn best, you must teach them in the way, or intelligence, they learn best in. The intelligences are as follows (Department of Natural and Cultural Resources, North Carolina Arts Council, A+ Schools Program, n.d.):

- Verbal-linguistic intelligence (*word smart* or *book smart*)
- Visual-spatial intelligence (*art smart* or *picture smart*)
- Intrapersonal intelligence (*self-smart* or *introspection smart*)
- Bodily-kinesthetic intelligence (*body smart* or *movement smart*)
- Interpersonal (*people smart* or *group smart*)
- Naturalist intelligence (*nature smart* or *environment smart*)
- Musical-rhythmic intelligence (*music smart* or *sound smart*)

Teaching using Gardner's theory is different than teaching the way it had been done in the past. For example, the following is a sample of teaching using bodily-kinesthetic intelligence:

I tell the students that our room is our database and they are all items in the database.

Then I ask for all the students with brown hair to stand up (this usually results in at least one good-humored discussion over whether a student has brown or blonde or black hair).

Then I ask for students with brown hair AND glasses, telling everyone else to sit back down. In my experience I almost always have 1–2 students who are still standing (if no one is left, it's a great teachable moment how sometimes we can narrow our results and get nothing, which means we have to broaden our search in some way—perfect transition to OR). I ask the students what happened to my results list and I can almost see lightbulbs go on as they shout "it got smaller" or "it narrowed!"

I have them sit down and ask for everyone wearing an earring to stand up.

Then I ask anyone wearing a necklace to join them.

Then I ask anyone wearing a watch or ring to join them.

When I ask what happened to my results list they realize that it got bigger or was broadened (sometimes no one else stands and it's a great opportunity to point out that this can happen in the library databases, too).

I ask them what earrings, necklaces, watches, and rings have in common (they're all accessories or jewelry) and use this to talk about using OR with related terms or synonyms and AND with different ideas.

It gets them physically moving and usually seems to really help them grasp the idea of AND and OR. I follow it up by doing a couple of sample searches in the database, showing them how it works there and then let them try it on their own. (Thompson, 2016)

If the students have bodily-kinesthetic intelligence and are being taught in that way, then they will be more engaged because the information will make more sense to them. One can best use this in a 15-week semester course. If the syllabus is divided such that every week a different intelligence is used as the basis of the lesson, then every week at least one part of the class will be getting the most learning out of the lesson.

Experiential Learning

Another underlying theme of this book is experiential learning. Experiential learning is simply defined as learning through experience (Kolb, 2014). The authors believe that the best way to engage students is to allow them to experience it themselves. Most librarians allot a certain percentage of their class time to "hands-on research." This represents an important component in student engagement. Student engagement is directly associated with allowing students to make connections through direct experience, for example, students doing their own database searches, seeing for themselves the key differences between newspapers, magazines, and academic journals. A perfect example of experiential learning is when Polger brings different periodicals to class to allow students to sift through and discover the differences between newspapers, magazines, and academic journals.

Experiential learning does occur outside class. Field trips, service learning, internships, externships, travel-abroad opportunities, and job shadowing allow students to experience what is taught in the classroom (Zhao & Kuh, 2004). Experiential learning opportunities are also known as high-impact educational practices (HIPs) (Riehle & Weiner, 2013). Examples of high-impact educational practices include first-year seminars, general education courses, learning communities, intensive writing courses, collaborative assignments and projects, undergraduate research, travel-abroad opportunities, service learning, community-based learning, internships, capstone courses, and projects (Kuh, 2008).

As library instructors, we are limited to one-shot classes or semester-long information literacy classes within the confines of a classroom. Many librarians collaborate with faculty who teach general education courses, first-year college composition classes, and first-year seminar classes, and they often target learning communities. In the library classroom, librarians use experiential learning methods to ensure students are actively applying the concepts discussed in class to the real world.

Kolb's Learning Styles Inventory

In order to best promote learner engagement, it is important to understand how they learn. According to David Kolb's learning styles inventory (Kolb & Kolb, 2005), learning occurs in a cycle that begins with concrete experience. Students begin to understand what is being taught by connecting to their life experiences. When teaching, librarians may want to connect new concepts with students' life experiences. As an example, students may not understand book or article citations, but explaining that citations might represent the same descriptive information that falls into a person's profile on Facebook might make it easier for them to make a connection and understand. After concrete experience, the next phase of learning is reflective observation. By showing instructional videos, students might be more engaged because they are watching how something is being done. As an example, Polger asked his "Freshmen Skills" students if they learned how to cook by watching YouTube videos or by watching their family cook. It appeared that watching YouTube videos was more popular than learning from watching their family. This is a form of reflective observation.

The next phase of learning is active experimentation. Active experimentation represents learning by "doing." This is conducted throughout library instruction classes when we turn over the computers to students to practice searching for their research topics. This piece of the learning styles inventory provides the most engagement because students are in a state of action because they are experimenting in the research process themselves (as opposed to having it demonstrated while they are passive observers). The last phase of Kolb's learning styles inventory, which might be the most uncomfortable, is abstract conceptualization. This phase of the learning styles inventory represents the need to learn new, abstract concepts that are unfamiliar to us. It may be termed "uncomfortable" because anytime we learn anything unfamiliar, it could make the learner feel awkward (Onwuegbuzie & Jiao, 1998). Some examples of this would be looking up a brand new word in a dictionary or reading the instructional manual of a new cell phone that is completely unfamiliar.

Questionnaire on Student Engagement in the Library Classroom

Between December 2014 and October 2015, the authors administered an anonymous questionnaire with 10 questions (see Appendix) that received Institutional Revenue Board (IRB) approval from both of their prospective colleges in the City University of New York (CUNY) system.

The first five questions focus on how academic librarians define student engagement, and the latter part of the questionnaire focuses on how academic librarians assess the practical nature of their engagement practices. The questionnaire was sent to seven different library listservs in Canada and the United States (CULIBS, the CUNY librarians listserv, the ALA listservs: prtalk; academicpr; acr-iglmo; ili-l; infolit; and the Medical Library Association's listserv: MEDLIB-L).

Polger and Sheidlower received approximately 900 responses over a nine-month period. In terms of the response rate, it is imperative to remember that some librarians are on multiple listservs simultaneously and might have received this questionnaire more than once.

This questionnaire does not serve to create a standardized definition of student engagement, but rather it focuses on librarians' attitudes and their perception of student engagement in the library classroom. Some of the data are qualitative; some of them are quantitative. The questionnaire explores the attitudes of the participants who were kind enough to volunteer their time in order to complete this questionnaire.

The questionnaire was targeted to academic librarians who actively teach in a library instruction program. We used it in order to ask participants their thoughts on what student engagement means to them, how they engage their students, the strategies they use, and some of their challenges, as well as exploring their understanding of words that are used to describe engagement. Because the librarians who answered the questionnaire were chosen as a convenient sample, the sample is not a representative one. While doing this work, we never intended on creating a final definition of engagement. Our specific intention was to explore what engagement means to academic librarians who teach and how they engage their students in their classes. The sample we culled mainly consists of those academic librarians who mostly teach one-shot library instruction sessions. As already written earlier, our data is both qualitative and quantitative, and as we analyzed the data, we sought to develop a working definition of student engagement based upon the participants' brainstorming of supplied keywords, which we found in the literature and that describe engagement. Our questionnaire should not be used as a standard since all students learn differently and all librarians teach differently.

Findings

Following are the findings of the first five questions of the questionnaire. The first five questions focus on understanding the demographic makeup of our respondents and how engagement was conceptualized. For question #1, of the approximately 900 responses, 36 percent were from public four-year colleges, 27 percent were from public two-year colleges, 35 percent were from private four-year colleges, and 2 percent were from private two-year colleges. There seems to be an even distribution of librarians from public and private colleges. The questionnaire responses follow. If you want to see the actual questionnaire, turn to the Appendix.

Figure 1.1 illustrates the breakdown of the type of academic library respondents work at.

Of the people who identified their age (Q#2), there were 65 fewer people than who identified where they work. This means that the actual count of librarians identifying their age was a total of 805 librarians. Of the librarians who answered the questionnaire, 150 are between ages 18 and 30. The 31- to 40-year-old group is the largest group of respondents with 228 people answering. The people who answered this survey aged between 41 and 50 number 190 librarians.

Respondents between ages 51 and 60 numbered 157 or 19.50 percent of the total. Seventy-eight librarians who are between 61 and 70 years old participated in the survey. The final category, librarians over the age of 71, consisted of two respondents. Figure 1.2 shows the breakdown of respondents' age ranges.

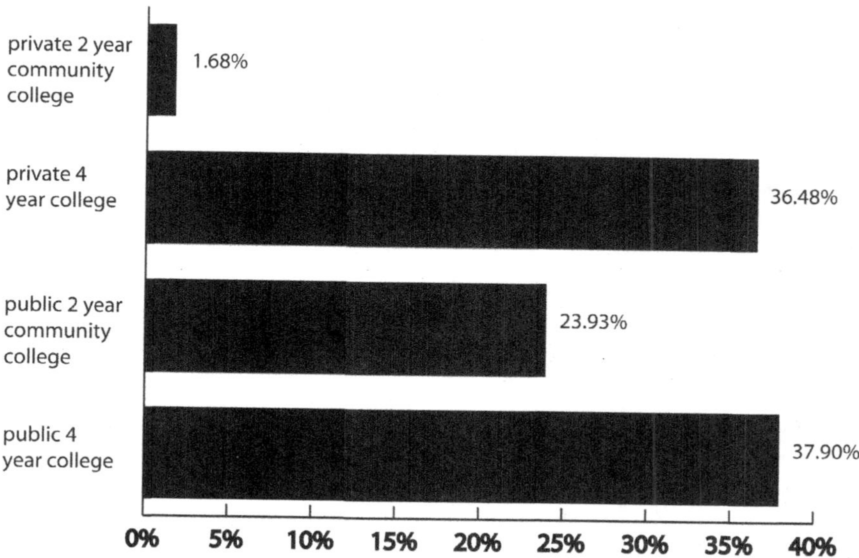

Figure 1.1 What Type of Academic Library Do You Work At?

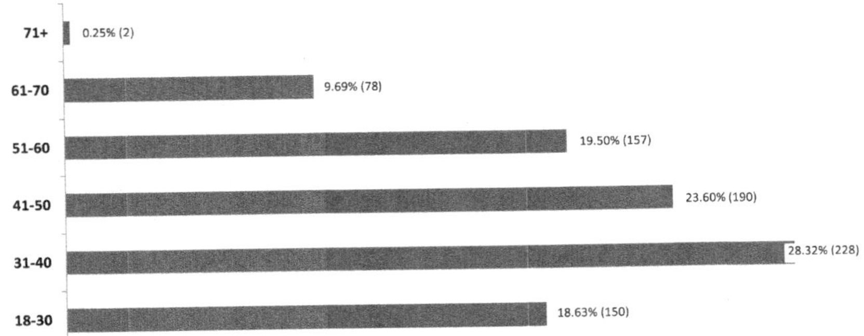

Figure 1.2 Age Category (not required)

The final demographic question (Q#3) asked was to try to determine how library instruction was taught. A total of 864 librarians answered this question, with six people choosing to skip it. Of those surveyed, the largest number of respondents we received, 722 librarians, teach one-shots. Both one-shots and "for-credit" classes are taught by 182 people. Only 10 people or 1.16 percent teach only "credit-bearing" classes. A total of 294 respondents, or 34.04 percent of people, were embedded in library instruction classes and working alongside faculty. This is the second largest group. Of those who answered, 13.77 percent of the surveyed or 119 academic librarians teach their "one-shots" online. Finally 71 people or 8.22 percent teach online "for credit." Figure 1.3 provides a breakdown of the different models of library instruction provided at various academic institutions.

As the literature confirms (Behrens, 1994; Grassian & Kaplowitz, 2001), library instruction is usually taught in the form of one-shot sessions (84 percent). However, some librarians report that they teach both one-shot and 15-week "for-credit" classes (21 percent). The number of librarians who report that they are physically embedded is 34 percent. On the other hand, 14 percent report providing library instruction online. The teaching of only 15-week "for-credit" classes is reported by 9 percent of our respondents (8 percent in person and 1 percent online).

When asked about defining "classroom engagement" (Q#4), respondents gave many answers. Words describing engagement were taken from library literature and from various thesauri. We had asked respondents to describe what engagement means in the library classroom. Academic libraries must engage with their users in order to grow and stay relevant. Engagement occurs throughout the library; it also happens from asking alumni for financial support, from answering a reference question, and even from lobbying

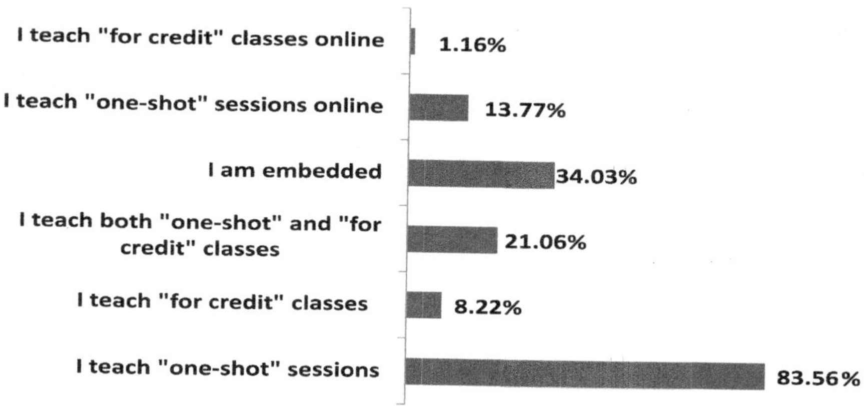

Figure 1.3 What Model of Library Instruction Do You Teach?

administrators for a budget increase. Our question was specifically targeted to engagement during library instruction sessions.

The eight most cited terms that describe that type of engagement are:

Connect   84%
Attention   83%
Interact   80%
Learn   75%
Motivate   74%
Dialogue   73%
Discuss   71%
Curiosity   68%

For the question (Q#5) on how librarians perceive students' feelings as they begin teaching, most librarians reported the following:

Students are apathetic   57%
Students are open to learning   54%
Students are open-minded   53%
Students look bored   46%

One set of questions the authors also asked was about best techniques to keep students engaged. These techniques are written about in Chapter 4. That set of questions will also be analyzed in that chapter. In the next chapter, the authors will discuss who our learners are and how their demographic characteristics affect how they are engaged and how they learn.

Questions 6 through 10 of the questionnaire will be examined in Chapter 4 as they pertain to teaching techniques, rather than conceptualizing the definition of student engagement.

In the next chapter, the generations of learners will be addressed so that it provides historical context to the diversity of learners across many generations.

The Generations of Learners

I want to be engaged as an adult who wants to learn, not as a child with attention issues.

—Anonymous survey respondent

As we wrote in Chapter 1, it is important to know who our learners are if we are to successfully engage them with our teaching. The American Library Association (ALA) insists that all students are treated equally. This idea of equal treatment is embedded in one of the basic, foundational ALA documents, the Code of Professional Ethics for Librarians, where it is written that, "We [librarians] provide the highest level of service to all library users [regardless of who they are] through appropriate and usefully organized resources; equitable service policies; equitable access; and accurate, unbiased, and courteous responses to all requests" (ALA, 2008). In addition, the *Library Bill of Rights* insists that "Libraries should provide materials and information presenting all points of view on current and historical issues. Materials should not be proscribed or removed because of partisan or doctrinal disapproval" (ALA, 1996). If the reader is a professional librarian and accepts and believes in these two documents, then it is helpful to understand whom we are teaching so we can better meet their needs.

It is a given that there are many ways to look at the world and at our students and none of them are necessarily wrong. According to an old saying, the glass could be "half empty" or "half full." Both of these viewpoints are correct. In the same way, each librarian can look at his or her patrons differently. For example, Hands (2015) in her analysis of the patrons she serves used information from the National Center for

Statistics and looked at her patrons numerically (pp. 3–4). Certainly, this makes sense when one is trying to allocate resources such as figuring out how many chairs and tables are needed in the library. However, when one is trying to teach students, a number does not tell you an awful lot. For example, how do you teach a 7? Is it different than teaching a 5,000.3? Besides being numbered differently, what are some of the other differences our students possess? We need to look at them less as an impersonal number and instead as some sort of a homogenous group possessing similar characteristics. Only then can we choose the proper motivational techniques required to reach each group. This chapter will show that "each of the various generational cohorts has its own values, motivations, and attitudes" (Wiedmer, 2015, p. 56). Wiedmer (2015) further observes that to teach a multigenerational group one must communicate with and motivate them based upon their preferences and characteristics and one must be flexible.

Not every student is in a class because he or she is intrinsically interested in the topic being taught by the professor. Some are enrolled in the course because it is a required course. Some are there because it was the only class open at that time and it fit their schedule. Some are there because they needed those credits to get a full financial aid package. There may be any of a large number of other reasons as well. The aforementioned reasons are some of the ones the authors have found the most at the City University of New York. Students are more than likely in the library classroom because they are required to be there by someone. Therefore, instruction librarians need to "sell" whatever they are teaching, however they are able to do so. Good salespeople usually know who their customers are. The idea of "selling" to the diversity of our learners will be discussed in Chapter 7. For example, Fromm and Garton (2013) wrote an entire book on marketing to a specific segment of the population, the millennials (see next section for who these people are). The techniques that compose the rest of the body of this book are the ways the authors believe that library lessons can be "marketed" to our students. This chapter takes a look at who these students are and analyzes this data.

Generations

Basing our analysis upon the work of Howe and Strauss (2000) of when students are born, we get a range of five student cohorts, laid out in Table 2.1, that might possibly be in our classrooms. In spite of the simplicity and popularity of this model, it has come under scrutiny and may not be correct (Hoover, 2009). Other researchers look at these groups differently even though the characteristics of many of them remain the same. For example, Wiedmer (2015) breaks our students down into six cohorts (see Table 2.2). Assuming that some college students are older retirees, then the oldest generation we might see in our colleges and universities in the early 21st century are from the G.I. generation. We could also work with some members of the silent generation or of the baby boomers or even some Gen X. Currently, traditional college students are from the millennial generation.

The G.I. Generation

The G.I. generation members, the group also known as "the greatest generation," were born between 1901 and 1924 (Howe & Strauss, 2000). The oldest members of this group have more than likely passed away. These oldest members fought in and won World War I and raised families during the Great Depression. The youngest members fought in and won World War II and were the grandparents of the baby boomers. Most of

Table 2.1 Names of Generations and Years Born According to Howe and Strauss (2000)

Name of Generation	Year Born
G.I. generation	1901–1924
Silent generation	1925–1942
Baby boomers	1943–1960
Gen X	1961–1981
Gen Y (i.e., Millennials)	1982–Present

Source: Adapted from Howe and Strauss (2000).

Table 2.2 Names of Generations and Years Born According to Wiedmer (2015)

Name of Generation	Year Born
Traditionalists	1900–1945
Baby boomers	1946–1964
Gen X	1961–1981
Gen Y	1980s–1990s
Gen Z	1995–2015

Source: Adapted from Wiedmer (2015).

them are probably retired and living on either Social Security or a pension or savings or all three. If they are in college today, they might be finishing up a graduate degree or just going to college for the fun of it. Of course, some could be either administrators or professors. The youngest of them, who had been born in 1924, currently, in 2015, is 91 years old.

The Silent Generation

The silent generation was born between 1925 and 1942 (Howe & Strauss, 2000). Members of this generation are, as of 2015, between 90 and 73 years old. The vast majority of them have more than likely retired. While some of them were born prior to the Great Depression, all of them, except the youngest, lived through the Great Depression and a majority of them fought in and won World War II. Some of them also fought during the Korean War. They could be either the grandparents or the parents of the baby boomers. If they are in college today, they might be either finishing up a degree or taking a course for fun or doing both. Like the G.I. generation, some could be either administrators or professors. Members of this group tend to be conservative, uneasy with the pace of social change, and in favor of limited government, except in the cases of Social Security and Medicare (Taylor, 2014, p. 33).

The Traditionalists

This group is also known as "Radio Babies, Builders, The Silent Generation, [G.I. Generation], and World War II Generation" (Wiedmer, 2015, p. 52) or veterans (Gibson, 2009). As mentioned under the sections "Silent Generation" and the "G.I. Generation," they have mostly aged out of both the population and the workforce. They like "conservative, hierarchical [environments] with top-down chains of command" (Wiedmer, 2015, p. 52). Their preferred method of learning is traditional, or to put it colloquially, the "sage on the stage" method (Wiedmer, 2015). Individually, they "[do] not like to challenge authority [and tend to be] very loyal, consistent, and conforming" (Stevens, 2010, p. 79). To them, education was not a right but rather a life goal (Gibson, 2009). Therefore, they value it highly. They get the most out of it when they get a detailed plan that includes the class's goals and its objectives (Gibson, 2009). Therefore, if you are teaching them, it is important to set these out at the start of the day's lesson.

The Baby Boomers

The baby boomers were born between 1943 and 1960 (Howe & Strauss, 2000). Some authors, however, place them between 1946 and 1964 (Wiedmer, 2015). They are, as of 2015, between 72 and 55 years old or between 69 and 51 (depending upon what dates you use). They lived through a very prosperous time in American history. They fought in Vietnam and they fought for civil rights, women's rights, and gay rights. The "post-war stress they experienced led them to being non-conformists, unlike their parents" (Stevens, 2010, p. 79), and so they saw and initiated a great many changes in the world, ranging from Woodstock to rioting in the streets. If they are currently in college, they could be doing almost anything from taking a degree to sharpen their skills and make them more marketable to finishing a degree to taking a course for fun, to administering the college, or to teaching in the college. Boomers tend to be "worried about retirement and gloomy about their lives" (Taylor, 2014, p. 33). Wiedmer, however, believes that they "have had good health, constitute the wealthiest generation, and optimistically view the world as improving over time" (2015, p. 52). Wiedmer (2015) accepts that there are two cohorts in the baby boomer generation: early boomers, who were born between 1945 and 1955, and late boomers, born between 1955 and 1964. The fear that Taylor (see above) observed seems to belong to members of the late boomers who are concerned about Medicare and Social Security (Adcox, 2015). Stevens writes of them as being "associated with optimism, team orientation, and personal gratification" (Stevens, 2010). At one point they were the largest generation consisting of 76 million people. In 2012, only 65 million of the original 76 million were left; however, 10 million immigrant boomers have raised their number to 75 million in total. Currently, millennials have surpassed them at 83 million souls. Unlike their parents—the traditionalists/veterans, silent generation, G.I. generation—boomers often easily accept education. Working with them in the classroom can be "tricky because they are competitive and are angered by any perceived threats to their authority" (Wiedmer, 2015, p. 53). In spite of this, Stevens notes that relationship building is important to them (2010, p. 79). Gibson notes that they learn best when they are given abundant amounts of positive reinforcement, when they are allowed to learn flexibly, and when they are given work to help them develop their skills (2009).

The Gen X

The members of Gen X were born between 1961 and 1981 (Howe & Strauss, 2000; Wiedmer, 2015). Gibson (2009) sees them as being born between 1960 and 1980. Therefore, as of 2015, they are between 54 and 34 years old according to the former two researchers or between 55 and 35 years old according to the latter researcher. The lives of Gen X as children were not as secure as the lives of the boomers. Because of a smaller birth rate, Gen X was termed "Gen Bust" and the "Forgotten Generation" (Wiedmer, 2015, p. 53; Lesonsky, 2016). They are known as the MTV generation, because they saw the beginning of music videos and the creation of hip-hop music.

Kersten (2002) explains that as a result of these life experiences, Gen X members tend to be skeptical, independent workers who highly value a balance between their work and their social life. They desire their time off more than extra pay or promotions and have little fear of changing jobs. In turn, they do not expect employer loyalty. This generation is shaped by a culture of instant results. They are comfortable with multitasking, are motivated to get the job done, value efficiency and directness, expect immediate responses, and look at education as a means to an end (Gibson, 2009, p. 37).

According to *Time* magazine, "Gen Xer" has come to mean "Gen Nester," as young parents invent new expedients (home schooling, telecommuting, etc.) to separate their children from whatever seems threatening and unreliable. "For many Gen Xers, starting and maintaining a stable family can be a . . . sense of pride—the pride you get for achieving something your parents did not" (Howe & Strauss, 2000, p. 56).

Like the baby boomers, some of Gen X may be attending colleges to sharpen their skills, some may be there just for personal fulfillment; and some may be professors or administrators. Since more Gen X members have bachelor's degrees than do baby boomers, they are considered the most educated generation; 31.1 percent boomers have bachelors and 34.6 percent of Gen X have that degree (New Strategist Editors, 2015, pp. 36–38). When they learn, they like things short and focused, and they get a lot out of the use of the Internet (Gibson, 2009). When teaching them, bullet points, outlines, and the like work very well.

The Millennials

The millennials (see also Chapter 6) were born after 1982 (Howe & Strauss, 2000). The oldest of them is 33 years old. They are also called

Gen Y (Tapscott, 2009, p. 17), "Echo Boomers, Millenniums or Millennials, Generation We, Internet Generation, Connect 24/7, and Leave No one Behind" (Wiedmer, 2015, p. 54). Gibson sees them as being born between 1981 and 2002 (2009, p. 37). This would make them between 34 and 12 years old. The 19-year-olds, who were born in 1996, make up the current class of traditional students were born in 1996. They have been studied extensively. They are the largest generation numerically. There are more of them than there are either baby boomers or Gen X (Fromm & Garton, 2013, p. 1). They are also the most educated generation having the most bachelor's degrees than either Gen X or boomers (New Strategist Editors, 2015, pp. 36–38). In point of fact "[in 2012, Millennials accounted] for the great majority of college students" (New Strategist Editors, 2015, p. 59).

While there are unique individuals in every group, as a whole, the millennials have the following qualities: they are digital natives (born to use technology and the Internet and are very comfortable with them); they were watched over by helicopter parents, many of whom followed them to college. Millennials "generally seek independent learning that implements thorough and comprehensive online research" (Wiedmer, 2015, p. 55). Millennials tend to be respectful of their elders, but not necessarily those elders who are in charge of them, such as teachers and librarians; they mature slowly; they are "conflict-averse; at ease with racial, ethnic, and sexual diversity; confident in their economic futures despite coming of age in bad times" (Taylor, 2014, p. 33).

Not everyone believes that millennial characteristics are inherent to that generation. Some have thought these characteristics are related to the students' socioeconomic level. Over the last decade, commentators have tended to slap the millennial label mainly on white, affluent teenagers who accomplish great things as they grow up in the suburbs, who confront anxiety when applying to super-selective colleges, and who multitask with ease as their helicopter parents hover reassuringly above them. The millennial label tends not to appear in renderings of teenagers who happen to be minorities, or poor, or who have never won a spelling bee. There are occasional exceptions, especially when people write about politics and are trying to identify a certain age group (Ramsey, 2015). Nor does the term often refer to students from big cities and small towns that are nothing like Fairfax County, Virginia. Or who lack technological know-how. Or who struggle to complete high school. Or who never even consider college. Or who commit crimes. Or who suffer from too little parental support. Or who drop out of college. However, aren't they millennials, too (Hoover, 2009)?

As a group, millennials are great believers in multitasking (Tapscott, 2009, p. 106). Unfortunately for them, "a growing body of research shows that juggling many tasks, as so many people do in this technological era, can divide attention and hurt learning and performance" (Richtel, 2011). On the whole, they tend to be less independent than previous generations.

Prensky sees them as becoming a totally different sort of learner than previous generations (2009). He believes that as digital natives they can use digital technology to become both "wiser and smarter" (Prensky, 2009, para 2). He defines "digital wisdom" as using digital technology to enhance problem solving. This makes the person using it smarter. Prensky says that this enhancement is all around us; for example, using the Internet to find out when a movie begins. This will free up the mind to do other things. Therefore, based upon Prensky (2009) we may conclude that when teaching millennials and Gen Z, using technology in a lesson will keep them more engaged. When planning to teach millennials "[t]echnology and social media create an atmosphere that encourages engagement and connectivity more than ever." The social media they preferred in 2011 were YouTube, Twitter, and Facebook (Ratliff, 2011).

Knowing who our students are means you can interact better with them. At the 2015 ALA conference in San Francisco, California, Sheidlower heard a 24-year-old librarian who works in a public library mention that his younger patrons saw him as old (personal communication, June 25, 2015). The older librarian, Sheidlower, recommended that he try breaking the ice with them and thereby personalize himself to them by using humor (one of the techniques found in this book and in Vossler and Sheidlower [2011]). Like Gen X, millennials like things in a lesson short and clear. They also like to work interactively in groups (Gibson, 2009).

Gen Z

While Wiedmer accepts that there is a Gen Z, born between 1995 and 2015 (2015), not every researcher recognizes them. For example, Gibson (2009) does not mention them. Like the other generations already mentioned, they are identified by multiple names: Wiedmer (2015), quoting both Menzies (2015) and Schroer (2015), names them: "Generation Z, Post-Millennials, Zs, Zers, iGeneration, Gen Tech, Gen Wii, Net Gen, Digital Natives, Gen Next, Post Gen, and Plurals."

Although the majority of Gen Z are still learning in K–12 environments (Renfro, 2012), the oldest group of them are starting college as traditional-age students (see next). They are very tech savvy with higher IQs than all previous generations (Renfro, 2012). They are very motivated by Web 2.0, preferring graphics, disliking "the sage-on-the-stage" lectures that the traditionalists preferred, and expecting instant feedback with customized content. The way they most like to learn is collaboratively, often using games (see Chapter 3) (Renfro, 2012). For librarians, it is important to note while Gen Z like technology, they ordinarily "do not take the time to determine the reliability of what they are researching on their technically-supported devices [however, like Gen Y, they are very comfortable with these devices]; therefore, in working with Gen Z individuals, teachers and other leaders should focus on helping them evaluate resources" (Wiedmer, 2015, p. 56). This important skill is reminiscent of the skills that the Association of College and Research Libraries requires of the information literate person. It can be identified in the *Framework for Information Literacy for Higher Education*, especially in the first frame, "Authority Is Constructed and Contextual" (ALA, Association of College and Research Libraries, 2015). It can also be identified in the *Information Literacy Competency Standards for Higher Education*, specifically in Standard Three: "The information literate student evaluates information and its sources critically" (ALA, Association of College and Research Libraries, 2000). Therefore, it is important that Gen Z spends time with librarians.

It is also important that librarians are given some professional development in teaching millennials and Gen Z since they learn differently than the way many librarians have learned. This may be because "41 percent of librarians are in their 50s" (Davis, 2009, p. 9) and are baby boomers. An example of such a professional development training was found at the fifth annual CUNY education conference held on May 8, 2009, at Lehman College in the Bronx. It was about teaching millennial learners, and through a day-long program of forums and posters, faculty shared how to teach millennials through different techniques and different theories.

Traditional-Age Students versus Nontraditional-Age Students

Traditional college-age students are defined as being "24 years or under" and nontraditional college-age students are defined as being "25 years or older" (Myers & Mobley, 2004). This means that traditional students are all millennials and as such addicted to multitasking. Traditional-age students may have come directly from high school after a short period working or after having done their version of either the "Grand Tour" or a "gap year." Nontraditional-age students come to college with more life experience than the traditional-age students. They may have raised a family, had a career, tried college and failed, and are there for the second time. They could be immigrants who were not able to go to college in their country of origin. Either type of students could be the first in their family to go to college. If they are the first students in their family to go to college, it is possible that they will be more interested/excited in being there than those students to whom going to college is a norm of family life and experience. But they may also need more help than the other students in the class because they don't know what to expect. As you teach your class, go slowly and repeat the main points several times. This will help them identify those main points more easily. It will also help multitasking millennials catch those ideas, if they are not paying attention.

The next chapter focuses on how to best engage different learner groups. Every learner is diverse and every learner connects with the concepts differently. The following chapter addresses the plethora of differences among different learning communities and will address how we can connect with their unique needs.

CHAPTER THREE

Examining Diverse Learning Groups

Everyone learns differently. There are so many external factors that affect learning and engagement.

—Anonymous survey respondent

It almost does not need to be stated that everybody learns differently. Chapter 2 covered students' generational differences and how this could affect how librarians teach. All differences influence both student learning styles and the ways through which faculty teach. Faculty teaching styles are not covered in this book because they have been addressed elsewhere (Cothran et al., 2005).

It is important to write about student diversity because as Parham observed, it "enriches [the library and] . . . contributes to the success and satisfaction of both library information seekers and information providers" (2006, p. 203).

Disabled Students

The year 2015 was the 25th anniversary of the Americans with Disabilities Act (the ADA). This law is important because it both defines who a disabled student is and sets up the relationship between the disabled student and the faculty member. The purpose of the ADA was to "[eliminate] discrimination against people with disabilities. It means that the United States, [through the Civil Rights Division of the Department of Justice] is working towards a future in which all the doors are open to equality of opportunity, full participation, independent living, integration and economic self-sufficiency for persons with disabilities" (Gupta, 2015). As quoted here, the ADA only covers people with disabilities. A "disability" is defined in the law as "a physical or mental impairment that substantially limits one or more major life activities, a person who has a history or record of such an impairment, or a person who is perceived by others as having such an impairment" (U.S. Department of Justice, n.d.). The disabled student must also self-identify to either the college or the professor. Additionally, his or her request for accommodation must be "reasonable." Reasonable means that it must be reasonably but not excessively affordable by the college and physically doable. For example, if you have a classroom without any seats and you have a student with a disability that does not let him or her stand for long periods of time and she or he self-identifies to you and requests a chair, it must be supplied to him or her, unless it would destroy a rare and expensive floor or carpet. If the student requested a solid gold chair, that would be prohibitively expensive and need not be supplied. A chair that floats in air would not exist technologically and at this time also need not be provided. This affects the main thesis of this book because the coauthors have supplied various strategies to engage students. Whichever one(s) the reader uses must be chosen with a disabled student in mind. To help the reader with this issue, whatever way the reader's institution schedules library lessons, the library lesson request form from other faculty should include space for the requesting teacher to identify disabled student(s) and his or her needs. The teaching librarian should then examine the lesson to make certain that however or whatever is being taught uses techniques that the entire class can use including any identified disabled students. For example, if one or more students are dyslexic, the lesson should not rely heavily upon needing to read quickly in class. Some disabilities are very easy to identify. For example, when one sees a student in a wheelchair, then one may guess that that student has a mobility disability.

However, there are also hidden disabilities such as epilepsy, dyslexia, and so on. These are disabilities that cannot be identified except when a student is suffering the consequences of the disability, such as when an epileptic has a seizure. When not seizing, it is impossible to look at someone and identify that person as an epileptic. As pointed out, during a seizure one can easily make that identification. Because of this, it is important to make certain that either your college's office of disabled students or the scheduling teacher notifies you of a student's special needs so that you get it correctly and teach properly. This is important because, excluding invisible disabilities, one cannot always identify a student's disability appropriately just by looking at him or her. For example, the aforementioned student in a wheelchair might not have the mobility disability that prevents him or her from putting one foot in front of the other but rather a problem with his or her balance or even a fear of standing.

According to the Individuals with Disabilities Education Act, also known as the IDEA, beginning at age 3, any public school student who requires special services must get an individualized education program (IEP; Stansberry, n.d.). This is mentioned because it has been Sheidlower's experience that freshmen often believe that the school and, therefore, you the librarian know about their disability when they show up at your college. Up until college or university, the IEP has automatically followed them through grades K to 12. It does not follow them to college and they are required under the ADA to self-identify their disability to the school and many of them do not realize this. One way to deal with this problem is to get your new disabled college freshmen involved with a library lesson that meets their needs. This can be done by holding an open lesson of basic information literacy for any and all disabled students. The librarian can then teach using techniques that work with the specific disabilities in the classroom (Sheidlower, 2008). If a representative from your college's office of disability is there, he or she can give the new students information about their program and you can give the students a basic information literacy lesson, thereby achieving two important tasks at once.

There are many different types of disabilities. They all have different characteristics and range from intellectual disabilities such as Down syndrome to physical disabilities such as epilepsy to learning disabilities such as central auditory processing disorder, to emotional problems, for example, phobias, to behavioral difficulties with Tourette syndrome (Westwood, 2009). All of these must be treated differently. This book can only mention them in passing. Westwood (2009) deals with them specifically.

Veterans

In the summer of 2014, Polger led a library orientation class targeted at incoming student veterans. As part of the class and tour, one of Polger's colleagues came over and explained to each of the five or six students on the tour that "we librarians can counsel you if you have PTSD and if you need someone to talk to, we can help you in the library." As expected, the students were uncomfortable and felt awkward that this librarian made the assumption that all student veterans had PTSD (post-traumatic stress disorder). Since Polger coordinated new student orientations, he later explained to his colleague the inappropriateness in making assumptions about students. It is very important to possess the skill of sensitivity when teaching to a specific target population. Employing sensitivity and avoiding assumptions represent basic tenets of good teaching practices. It seems like there is more to be said about teaching veterans than if they have PTSD and thus attention disorder—many are older and coming back to school, have families, and perhaps working full time; many have disabilities, and may feel persecuted or out of step with civilian life, but may be pretty savvy with technology.

Gay, Lesbian, Bisexual, Transgender, Questioning, Intersex Students

Considering that the gay rights movement only began in the summer of 1969 with the Stonewall Riots in New York City's Greenwich Village, the field of librarianship was on the forefront of this movement. Its earliest gay rights organizing most likely occurred as early as the fall of 1970 when "a group of gay librarians formed a caucus within the American Library Association (ALA) [in order] to do something about the literature and the problems in the profession" (Kniffel, 1999, p. 74). The following year at the ALA conference in Dallas, the group began in earnest holding both serious events and less serious ones. An example of a serious one was a talk by "Michael McConnell, who had lost his librarian job when he wanted to be open as a gay person, and he was fighting his case in both the federal courts and in the American Library Association" (Kniffel, 1999, p. 74). Less serious but better attended was a kissing booth where one could both kiss and "Hug a Homosexual" (Kniffel, 1999, p. 74). Yet, in spite of all this early agitation, except for news reports, such as a *Life* magazine photographer taking pictures, and some local television coverage (Kniffel, 1999, p. 76), very little came out of this protest and except for the publication of subject headings by the Library of Congress using the term "Gay." Nothing about the LGBT community was published in the field of library science until 1990 (Gough & Greenblatt, 1990).

Despite the fact that as early as the mid-1980s, libraries in institutions of higher education were starting to be mentioned by educational reformers (American Library Association, Association of College and Research Libraries, Presidential Committee on Information Literacy 1989) and in spite of bibliographic instruction having been developed in the 19th century and revived in the 1960s (Hopkins, 1982), Gough and Green-blatt's (1990) volume does not even address this earlier idea of biblio-graphic instruction, let alone the latter concept of information literacy.

Martin and Murdock (2007) quoted Martin Garner who wrote that "in the literature of library and information science, the information needs of the lesbian, gay, bisexual, and transgender . . . community have been dis-cussed infrequently, studied less, and never treated in their totality" (p. 21).

Farmer, McKay, and Tsakiris (2014) have found that people trust peo-ple who look like themselves. In other words, people trust members of the group they belong to. How can that translate into engagement? It means that whomever you teach, you try to connect to them on their level even if you belong to another group. For example, when Sheidlower was a volunteer docent in the education department at the American Museum of Natural History, his supervisor, M. Ransom, narrated the following incident during a training session (personal communication, Septem-ber 25, 1979). According to his supervisor, another docent had demon-strated an African game made of small rings and a stick. The docent told the class, a class which came from a poorer school in Harlem, that they could create the game with a stick, a piece of rope, and some of their mother's napkin rings. The problem, according to Ransom, was that these children's parents were poor and they probably did not have napkin rings, which is a luxury product. Ransom's suggestion was to use the cardboard inside of a roll of paper towels and cut that up into rings. The children would have had access to that but probably not napkin rings.

How does this relate to teaching students who are different from us? Students have to be approached at their own level with familiar refer-ences. This is particularly important because as McDowell (2000) observed in the case of gay, lesbian, bisexual, transgender, questioning, intersex (LGBTQI) students, "College is an important period in the iden-tity development of LGBT[QI] students" (p. 71). Therefore, if one is teach-ing a class solely consisting of LGBTQI students, then if one needs to give an example of a kiss, one might give an example of a kiss between two acknowledged gay actors such as Jim Parsons and Matt Bomer or Ellen DeGeneres and Rosie O'Donnell and not two heterosexual actors such as Anne Hathaway and Hugh Jackman. While doing this, it is important to "remember to include terminology specific to particular ethnic or cultural groups among your student body, bearing in mind that sexual and gender roles can vary from society to society and that terminology may not be directly transferable" (McDowell, 2000, p. 81).

When teaching anyone anywhere on campus, the professor, in order to engage the students must remember that, the classroom—the place on campus reserved for the free and respectful exchange of ideas—should provide an oasis from [a] seemingly constant barrage of anti-LGBT harassment, violence, and invalidation [which is found on campus]. Unfortunately, this is not the case. In 1993 the Select Commission on Lesbian, Gay, and Bisexual Concerns at the University of Minnesota reported testimony from undergraduate and graduate students who described their experience in the classroom in pursuit of their academic program of study. Students told of occasions when faculty made derogatory jokes, minimized or denied the contributions of LGBT people, and denied, made light of, or dismissed as irrelevant the sexual orientation of artists, scientists, or historical figures. Students also reported incidents of professors making overtly hostile or demeaning comments, including some implying that violence against LGBT people is justified and deserved. (Renn, 1998, pp. 231–232)

Renn also notes other studies of homophobia and heterosexism on other campuses such as at both Brown and Oberlin (1998, p. 232). These studies have the same outcomes as the Minnesota study discussed earlier but also suggest that, by not acting against homophobes on campus, even the most tolerant of colleges can seem threatening.

One might use words and examples from LGBTQI culture anyway. The more silent academia is in relationship to the existence and the legitimacy of homosexuality and homosexuals, the more the academy impacts negatively on both LGBTQI students and heterosexual students. McDowell (2000) has written about how whenever the academy legitimates:

heterosexism—the belief in the inherent superiority of heterosexuality, and the assumption that everyone is or should be heterosexual. The heterosexist classroom environment not only fails to challenge the climate of bigotry [including but not limited to racism, ageism, ableism, antisemitism, and islamophobia, to name but a few examples] that exists on the campus but it also provides ideological support for that bigotry and homophobia. (p. 73)

McDowell (2000) has found that "LGBT[QI] students can benefit from a broad range of instructional strategies, including displays, pathfinders and workshops" (p. 78). Displays can be used to teach not only students but also library workers and librarians. An example where this was done was at Trent University in the province of Ontario, Canada (McDowell, 2000, 78). Whatever techniques one uses to teach LGBTQI students, one should remember to try to acknowledge, affirm, and "support these students *as LGBT individuals*" (Chesnut, 1998, p. 222).

An example of an academic library pathfinder created for LGBTQI students is the LibGuide for LGBT people found at COM college in Texas (Park, 2015). McDowell (2000, p. 80) suggests that "a specialized LGBT library workshop can be part of a regular schedule, tied in with LGBT-awareness events or other functions organized by students or faculty, or created for a particular course."

One's sexuality may not seem important to some readers. However, Anderson (quoted in, 1997, p. 141) wrote that "[i]n fact sexuality is very salient in the workplace, as we now know from research on sexual harassment and are beginning to learn from studies of gay and lesbian experiences at work." This leads to the idea that another way to engage LGBTQI students is to come out as a faculty member in the classroom, if you can and it is true. Students often look to faculty to model parts of their lives from them. A student who is in the closet could find having a LGBTQI professor as someone to look up to (McNaron, 1997). While one might think that this is mainly true for students in a lower grade and that college students already have created a self-identity, Fine (2011) observed that "[a]lthough the out students interviewed were comfortable with their sexual identity, heteronormativity still affected their lives" (p. 533). In other words, the gay professor in the closet is the character model for the gay student looking to have a LGBT sexual identity while being perceived as heteronormative otherwise.

Additionally, McNaron observed in her 1997 study of LGBT faculty that the ability "to see oneself mirrored in the society to which one gives one's allegiances and energies [in this case the academy] is important because without this fundamental validation, most of us will not thrive, no matter how hard we try to adapt and adjust to the system." (p. 199).

According to academic librarian Rachel Wexelbaum at Saint Cloud University in Saint Cloud, Minnesota,

> Student engagement has to do . . . with how motivated a student is to participate in all that the campus has to offer, from their regular coursework to extracurricular activities.
>
> They are "overrepresented" in our Honors program, and are more likely to visit the library than other students. Those who have reached a certain point in their identity development also go through an "activist" phase where they get involved in student organizations—LGBT and otherwise—to pursue their causes. Those LGBT who do not do well in school are usually those who have overscheduled themselves, or those who are suffering

from the effects of stress, or both. I have research articles to back this up if you would like them.

Student engagement in a library instruction class, to me, means that students come to library instruction with a research topic in mind, they ask questions, and they share their findings with me or the class as a whole. They will look at me, and not look at their phones or other devices, when I do teach. This applies to LGBT students as well as other students.

If I do a one-shot library instruction session, I ask the instructor to collect questions and/or research topics from the students ahead of time. I type out the questions and pass them back to the students, so that they know that I will be responding to their questions during the session, and they can use the list of questions as a "checklist" or write the answers underneath. I will stop at a certain point and ask them if there were any questions I did not answer, or if they have any more questions that they thought of during the session. When doing demos, I will use their research topics to demo online searching. I will ask them whose topic it is, and to follow along because they are getting a little head start on their research! Of course, I also give the students plenty of time to do the online searching during the class, and I walk around and give them one on one assistance.

When I see students making connections during library instruction, where they persist and learn from trial and error in order to tweak a research question or locate more specific resources, that is a measure of engagement. When students actually leave the library instruction classroom to go find the book they located in the catalog and return to the classroom with it, that is super engagement! When the students talk with each other about their research, and seek help from each other, that is also super engagement.

In communicating with students, it is recommended to avoid assumptions of anyone's gender identity or sexual orientation. It is not important (in a classroom context) to classify one's gender identity or sexual orientation when teaching. In Polger's freshmen skills class, he discusses the importance of thinking differently about how we classify people in their profession. Examples brought into class are using "police officer" as opposed to "policeman," using "firefighter" as opposed to "fireman," and using "flight attendant" as opposed to either "stewardess" or "steward."

When giving research topic examples in information literacy classes, librarians need not assign a gender when discussing doctors or nurses, counselors or social workers, engineers or computer scientists. Using "them" as opposed to "he/him, she/her" is more inclusive and rejects the need to use gender as an adjective.

Given the fact that our culture is heteronormative, it is important to discuss current topics that affect the LGBT community such as gender-neutral restrooms, physical violence in the transgender community, inequality for transgendered persons of color, marriage equality, LGBT rights, and other timely or relevant topics that are important for the LGBT community.

It also brings validity and legitimacy to the experiences of LGBT people, even though there might not be any LGBT learners in the classroom. It also provides an inclusive environment where discussion is welcome.

Since both authors identify as members of the LGBT community, we believe it is important to engage students with discussions about current topics in the news. By bringing these topics out in the open, it helps to bring awareness to the entire classroom. Some librarians avoid teaching research topics such as cancer because some students may have a lost a family member to cancer and librarians may not want to make some students uncomfortable. If librarians discuss issues such as violence in the transgender community, it might make other cisgender students feel uneasy but it recognizes the diversity of our human population. By hiding (or avoiding) any sensitive topics, librarians are doing a disservice and ultimately self-censoring themselves. Ignoring current issues can cause the lesson to lose a certain immediacy, making it duller, and giving students a reason to be disengaged.

English Language Learners

As Polger teaches required information literacy and freshmen skills classes to speakers of other languages, he has learned that it is best to engage students by using plain language, avoid jargon, enunciating words, and using comparisons when teaching. It is doubly challenging for instructors who are teaching content having to making certain that the language of instruction is understood as well.

Since Polger does not hold a master's degree in Teaching English to Speakers of Other Languages (TESOL), he is not as experienced at engaging students with the content of the lesson and the English language. He recognizes that he does not possess the skills and knowledge to teach the content (information literacy) with the techniques needed to successfully teach learners whose native language is not English. He finds it challenging as he sometimes feels disconnected from the class due to the language barrier. He does use other techniques (discussed elsewhere in the book) to teach them, but he is uncertain as to their efficacy.

Students of Color

According to Lynch (n.d.), 86.78 percent of the librarians working in academic libraries in 1998 were white and only approximately 6 percent were black. According to Tatum (1997, p. xv), this has a negative consequence in racially mixed classrooms because white librarians and teachers lack an interpretive framework that would help them understand the development of the identity of black students. Because we all live in a racist society, we are both victims and perpetrators of cultural racism. Tatum further defines "cultural racism" as "the cultural images and messages that affirm the assumed superiority of Whites and the assumed inferiority of people of color." (1997, p. 6). An example of this might be if one sees a black male teenager making a lot of noise, one might react with, "oh that's the way they all are." But if one sees a white male teen doing the exact same thing, this might cause the reaction, "Oh well, boys will be boys."

While it is true that many whites are not actively racist, with active racism meaning that they consciously act in a racist manner, nonetheless some are passively racist. This is defined by Tatum (1997) as:

> more subtle and can be seen in the collusion of laughing when a racist joke is told, of letting exclusionary hiring practices go unchallenged, of accepting as appropriate the omissions of people of color from the curriculum, and of avoiding difficult race-related issues. (p. 11)

Tatum (1997) finally sums up the issues in dealing with students of all sorts as follows: "How do we create and sustain school environments that affirm identity, build community, and cultivate leadership in a way that supports the learning of all students?" (p. 218. These needs are more fully addressed in critical race theory (CRT), a framework that looks at ways that race and racism affects society and scholarship (Yosso, Smith, Ceja, & Solórzano, 2013). According to Hall and Martin (2013), CRT

> [r]equires individuals to recognize their own personal investment in oppressive institutional and ideological structures through five central themes: (1) the centrality of race and racism; (2) the challenge to dominant ideology; (3) a commitment to social justice and praxis; (4) the centrality of experiential knowledge; and (5) an historical and interdisciplinary perspective. (p. 95)

Using CRT as a framework, Hall and Martin (2013) studied how to better engage and retain both African American students and students who are "products of the hip-hop culture" (p. 94); these are probably both millennial and Gen X students. Hall and Martin did a case study of the use of hip-hop as a style of pedagogy in several English classes with the same professor at an unidentified historically black college and university. They then proceeded to connect this form of "hip-hop pedagogy" to CRT (Hall & Martin, 2013). Hip-hop pedagogy was found by these two researchers to engage African American students.

This use of hip-hop pedagogy to infuse education can be found not only at the level of higher education, but also at lower educational levels as, for example, in the many educational ways that the Pulitzer Prize–winning and Tony-winning hip-hop Broadway musical *Hamilton* is used. *Hamilton* has a book, lyrics, and music by Lin-Manuel Miranda (Hamilton, n.d.). Miranda based *Hamilton* upon a scholarly, over 800-page biography, written about the first treasury secretary of the United States, Alexander Hamilton, by Ron Chernow (2005). Miranda wrote it in hip-hop because he felt that this was a "wonderful language for our revolution. We need a revolutionary language to describe a revolution" (PBS NewsHour, 2015). This desire for immediacy led the show to be cast by a diverse group of actors: blacks, Latinos, Asians, whites, and so on. Miranda explained this casting choice as follows:

> I think one of our overarching goals with this show is—with any show—is, you want to eliminate any distance between your audience and your story. And so let's not pretend this is a textbook. Let's make the founders of our country look like what our country looks like now. (PBS NewsHour, 2015)

This has been so successful that the Rockefeller Foundation has invested $1.5 million to help New York City school children from Title I schools attend the play. Title I schools are schools with a large number of students from low-income families and homes and therefore these are the schools that receive financial aid (Kendall, 2016). Miranda's attention to the historical facts combined with the play's language has been so successful that it has become the basis of many lesson plans (Schulten, Gross, & Gonchar, 2016).

Additionally, hip-hop pedagogy fights the historical racism of America's first school created to teach American Indians (indigenous people) "properly," the Carlisle Indian Industrial School (Emdin, 2016). Founded in the 19th century in Carlisle, Pennsylvania, the Carlisle Indian Industrial School tried to educate the Native American by using authoritarian techniques to force these indigenous peoples to become like the white man. Emdin observed that in doing so "[the students] were stripped of their culture and traditions [by the teachers because these were] considered primitive and inferior" (Emdin, 2016, p. 4).

Emdin argues that because of this connection, the "correct" way to teach youth of color, whom he terms "neoindigenous," is to "make some sense of the [urban] youth['s] realities, place, and space" (2016, p. 26). This requires, according to Emdin (2016), approaching the students as people influenced by their cultural identity. Emdin terms this "reality pedagogy" (p. 27) and defines it as follows: "Reality pedagogy is an approach to teaching and learning that has as a primary goal of meeting each student on his or her own cultural and emotional turf" (Emdin, 2016, p. 27). In order to do this and to teach directly to the students, one must be connected with them emotionally. This allows movement "from the classroom (place) to the spaces where the students are" (Emdin, 2016, p. 37). Emdin (2016) summarizes this as

> an approach to urban education that benefits the two most significant parties in the traditional school—the student and the teacher—an approach to teaching and learning that not only considers what is right for students, but what makes the teacher most effective and fulfilled. (p. 42)

A part of reality pedagogy that can be used with these same urban students is called by Emdin "pentecostal pedagogy" (2016, p. 50). Emdin (2016) further writes that

> [p]entecostal pedagogy gleans teaching practices from the black church and is a necessary model for teachers charged with engaging urban youths of color in classrooms but who have no training in what it means to be neoindigenous and alienated from traditional school culture. (p. 50)

This pentecostal pedagogy is similar to hip-hop pedagogy. It is also the source of hip-hop pedagogy (Emdin, 2016, p. 54). In hip-hop music, the rapper is trying to "MC or move the crowd [which is about being] able to share information, spark thinking, invoke dialogue, and keep an audience engaged" (Emdin, 2016, p. 52). Both the rapper and the preacher

> use call-and-response (e.g. asking the congregation the question "Can I get an amen?" and waiting for the audience to put their hands up and respond) to ensure the crowd is engaged, use the volume of their voice . . ., actively work the room, and make references to contemporary issues or respond to cues in the immediate environment to enliven their [lessons]. (Emdin, 2016, p. 52)

This can be easily translated into the library classroom.

While call-and-response in a church service can be a complicated set of rhythms and words, at its simplest, it is stepping out of your role as teacher and asking students questions they all need to answer. For example, "What are the Boolean connectors?" Let them all yell out the answer and then, if it is correct have them all say together, "and, or, not." The issue of the change in the volume of your voice is simply making certain that you are not speaking in a monotone. Actively working the room is walking around and interacting with the students. Making references to contemporary issues could be taking a national news story and having students research a part of it as an information literacy exercise.

Now that we have identified who our students are, the next chapter explores the many ways we can engage our learners.

CHAPTER FOUR

Teaching Techniques That Engage Learners

Teaching is a performance, it's exhausting and gratifying at the same time. To teach effectively is both an art and science. The more I teach, the better I become.

—Anonymous survey respondent

Introduction

The following chapter is the largest and arguably the most important chapter in this book. It reports on the data culled from our questionnaire ($N = 900$) that we administered in December 2014. Half of the questionnaire reports on how librarians conceptualize "engagement" and the other half of the questionnaire discusses various practical teaching strategies librarians use to engage their learners. In addition, this chapter also addresses further conceptions of engagement from our interviews conducted with over 20 instruction librarians.

This chapter focuses on the different techniques librarians use to best capture students' attention and to keep them engaged and motivated to learn. "The key to becoming an effective educator is acknowledging the differences between students and teacher and adjusting one's teaching accordingly, which often requires nontraditional approaches to teaching and learning" (Emdin, 2016).

Like many librarians who provide classroom instruction, Polger is very invested in attempting to engage students. Librarians' time with students is often limited, so Polger tries to make the most of it. To this end, Polger has used small group activities, student presentations to the rest of the class, watching a short clip from a TV show or movie about libraries or information and discussing it as a group, and a library activity based on a reality TV show, among other methods. These all have had varying levels of success depending on the class, and Polger has found there is no simple answer to one thing that consistently works in achieving student engagement.

Polger will often ask students what they learned from the class, and what they would like to know more about. He has tried assessment methods like pre- and posttests, but finds that these are too rigid and focused on the quantifiable to meaningfully address something as messy and complicated as engagement and learning. Providing time for student reflection and asking their thoughts at the end of a session has been beneficial for both the students and the instructor. When possible, Polger also takes time after a class to think about how it went and what he could improve on next time, which includes the level of student engagement that he has observed.

Teaching Techniques

In our questionnaire, approximately 900 respondents answered the question on techniques librarians use to engage learners during classes. The following subheadings represent different strategies librarians use.

Humor

Approximately 80 percent of respondents to our questionnaire used humor in their classes as a way to engage learners. Historically, pedagogy was perceived of as being a very serious occupation and humor was rarely used as a teaching tool; however, in the 1950s and 1960s, it began to be used as such a tool (Vossler & Sheidlower, 2011, p. 23). By the 1980s and during the 1990s, humor and other forms of entertainment began being used fairly frequently in order to teach (Postman, 2006; Vossler & Sheidlower, 2011). As early as 1973, this combination of education and entertainment was described by a new word: edutainment (Edutainment, n.d.).

Romal (2008) identified in studies dating from the 1990s to around 2005 that humor is one of the positive traits found in the most effective teachers. Humor, in addition to storytelling, can be used in the classroom to "[diffuse a student's] negativity or anxiety" (Emdin, 2016, p. 58). Current educational research "shows that humor in the classroom creates less threatening social scenarios and makes students more comfortable communicating with the teacher" (Emdin, 2016, p. 70).

There have been multiple research studies of humor and education from both a pedagogical point of view (e.g., Kaplan & Pascoe, 1977; Torok, McMorris, & Lin, 2004; Ziv, 1976) and a psychological point of view (e.g., Chapman & Crompton, 1988; Frymier & Weser, 2001). However, due to the fact that they are studying different things in relationship to humor and learning, such as the relationship of humor to the recall of facts or the relationship of humor to creativity, these studies do not all agree conclusively that humor helps students learn (Vossler & Sheidlower, 2011). It has been noted, nonetheless, that humor reduces classroom anxiety (Korobkin, 1988). In our experience, however, humor helps students learn from librarians by making the librarian more approachable and less of an authority figure.

Vossler and Watts (2011) have noted that "information literacy instruction should be as much about building bridges with students as it is about imparting useful information and skills. Entertaining while educating (edutaining) promotes student attention and helps build a positive learning environment." When librarians are more approachable, students are less afraid, or put another way, they are more comfortable approaching the librarian for help. Another thing that humor does is it stimulates the class's attention. "Laughter wakes up the classroom. More oxygen enters the blood during a good laugh and a variety of muscles react making your students more alert" (Arnsan, 2000, p. 54). Vossler and Sheidlower (2011, p. 10) also noted that humor can be used to "gain . . . and maintain . . . students' attention."

Library anxiety is an accepted part of the theory and practice of library science (Onwuegbuzie, Jiao, & Bostick, 2004).

Whether or not . . . library anxiety is to blame, there is a consensus that students in the library instruction classroom are prone to some kind of aversive emotional state, such as anxiety, stress, poor morale, or some combination thereof, and that humor is the antidote: "anxiety levels in [an] undergraduate class decreased by almost two standard deviations [when humor was used]." (Vossler & Sheidlower, 2011, p. 9)

There are many styles of humor out there. For example, Gracie Allen and Tina Fey (if the reader doesn't know who either of these people are, it is strongly recommended that they go to YouTube and see some samples of their work) both approach comedy differently. Therefore, when and if the reader chooses to use humor to help engage students, the reader should prepare to do this by first deciding what sort of humor he or she does best and then she/he should create a lesson plan with the jokes or humor outlined before using it. Additionally, the lesson should be tested out on either a family member or a colleague to make certain that the humor works and is funny. Polkinghorne (2015) describes several techniques from the performing arts that can help you create these lessons.

Almost any kind of joke can be used to engage a class. The humor works best if it relates to the topic being taught. For example, one could start a physics lesson about absolute zero by observing that "Absolute zero is cool" (Wiatco Internet Services, n.d.). However, it is important to remember that when planning to use a joke or any sort of humor "it is imperative that risqué or hostile humor never be directed at students" (Vossler & Sheidlower, 2011, p. 19). This is important because if the humor is aimed at a specific student, then the class might sympathize with the student and the professor could possibly lose the class's goodwill. Instead, if the humor must be aimed at a person, one can use someone who is not in either the room or the school and couldn't be there, such as King Henry VIII. One can also target the humor at a rival school or sports team. Humor can also be used as an icebreaker in the classroom (Emdin, 2016, p. 56).

Librarians also sometimes use whimsy and word puns to help themselves remain engaged in their teaching and even in their scholarly writing. Two examples of this are found in Stebbins (2015). One is found in the subtitle of Stebbins's book. The title is very plain and simple: *Finding Reliable Information Online.* On the other hand, the subtitle is more whimsical: *Adventures of an Information Sleuth.* While the title could, of course, have been supplied by the publisher's marketing department, the titles of the chapters were probably supplied by the author. Chapter 4 of Stebbin's book is titled with a "straight out" pun: "Word of mouse." This pun may have been created by Stebbins to help keep her attention on her task of writing the book.

Sheidlower has found in his teaching that a moderate dose of "shock" content helps to grab the attention of a lethargic class. For example, Sheidlower often discusses the use of virtual private networks and how they change the "location," that is, the IP address of the computer from the student's home or work to a campus IP address, thereby making database access appear as if it were free. He uses this time to discuss privacy and illegal use of the Internet. Sheidlower does this with a simple reference to a plausible current event scenario with which everyone is familiar.

According to a colleague, students sit up and take notice because they are experiencing a level of anxiety and discomfort, and Sheidlower feels that because they are uncomfortable, they become engaged with the material. The scenario joke is to explain that IP addresses are not private (as he provides a short one- two-sentence discussion of the Patriot Act). This is followed by explaining that the FBI can use these IP addresses, for example to track potential bomb-making activities, or currency counterfeiting schemes, or Web-based discussions in which public acts of violence are suggested or threatened. He assures student that they can continue to chat with friends about their mutual love of target practice or their irritation with airport security. There will be smiles of recognition in the class, because everyone feels irritation with airport security, and because there will no doubt be people in the class who enjoy guns recreationally, or who hunt, or who have strong views about the country's gun laws.

From that point forward, it is likely that students will be paying closer attention to his instruction, wondering what he may say next.

Vossler and Sheidlower (2011) have observed that if the reader wants to teach with humor, he or she should open the class humorously to set the tone. This is important because as Vossler and Sheidlower (2011, p. 54) noting that students have identified "sexual humor, ethnic humor, and aggressive or hostile humor as the most unacceptable forms of humor" (Vossler & Sheidlower, 2011, p. 41).

Therefore, the teacher needs to choose the correct type of humor, namely, puns, slapstick, and satire. McClennen and Maisel (2014) have observed that satire works very well with the millennials. They give numerous examples of this from both *The Daily Show with Jon Stewart* and *The Colbert Report*. Since these clips are both political and satirical, one could build an information literacy lesson in current American history, in political science, in journalism, in economics, in current world history, or even in linguistics (the relationship of Colbert and report [the silent "T" that Stephen Colbert uses in both his name and his report]).

If the reader decides to use humor as a teaching tool in the college classroom because it helps students learn or because it helps students remember or perhaps because it helps reduce classroom anxiety and the reader desires to find some examples of how to teach using humor, then both Berk (2002, 2003) and Vossler and Sheidlower (2011, pp. 61–123) give good, practical examples of how to use comedy in college classrooms. Berk more generally concentrates on using humor to teach statistics and Vossler and Sheidlower's examples are related to library science, specifically to teaching information literacy. These two sets of examples can be easily adapted by others for their classrooms.

"Real-World" Examples

Approximately 84 percent of librarians use real-world examples when teaching. Connecting the class content to real-world examples not only makes the class more accessible but also connects abstract concepts to the real-world examples that may make learning easier. For example, Polger shows Facebook profiles and illustrates that each of the fields of a Facebook record can resemble the fields of a library catalogue record. In addition, by showing Twitter hashtags and explaining the use of a hashtag, the difference between keywords and subject headings can be discussed. Polger often explains that subjects are more "official" (avoiding the term "controlled vocabulary") and keywords are more "unofficial" and user-driven. Polger then holds up various pieces of realia like his multicolored backpack with the JanSport brand name. Students are asked to call out keywords/hashtags that come to mind when they see the backpack. Polger demonstrates that each student may have different keywords that describe the backpack. In this example, some students call out "tie dye," "multicolor," "schoolbag," "backpack," or "JanSport."

For citations (books or articles), the Facebook profile example demonstrates that the profile is not the actual person but a description of the person, like a book or article record is not the actual book or article, but a description of it.

Class Activities

According to the responses to our questionnaire, 80 percent of librarians create an environment where class activities are used to engage learners. Librarians reported that creating activities such as group discussion, database searching activities, exploring research topics using Google, or verifying facts comparing Wikipedia and subscription databases are examples Polger uses in his classes. If the librarian is talking for 1 hour nonstop, the students will doze off and become disengaged.

In one of Polger's class activities, he asks students to identify their favorite celebrity on Wikipedia. He asks them to print out the first page of the Wikipedia page and identify three facts about the person on Wikipedia. After identifying the three facts, learners are asked to search the subscription-based academic databases the college subscribes to so they can verify the facts. This involves coming up with keywords and terms in order to verify the information found on Wikipedia. This activity engages students individually since they feel that they are on a scavenger hunt to verify facts.

Another activity used in Polger's information literacy classes is the analysis of different newspapers. Using a real-life example of the Katie Holmes and Tom Cruise divorce in 2012, Polger selected different newspapers that reported the event and asked learners to read the newspapers and compare the language, words, and tone of each article. Learners were able to identify the difference between more credible newspapers such as the *New York Times* versus more "tabloid-style" newspapers such as the *New York Post*.

Polger also brings copies of newspapers, magazines, and academic journals to class and asks students to take notes on the use of images, whether the publication is considered "research," whether the author is a paid staff, the number of pages per article. Learners get into groups of three and discuss the differences between the types of publications and this activity helps them distinguish the differences between the three types of periodicals. It also introduces a discussion of the differences between peer review and editorial review. More broadly, it also helps develop a discussion of what scholarship is, the politics of academic publishing, and the fact that academics don't get paid for their scholarly work. Lastly, students are shocked to learn that academic journal publishers charge back universities (who employ these scholars) with expensive annual subscriptions so that scholars can access their own articles.

Breaking Up the Lesson

In her article, "How to Teach in an Age of Distraction," Sherry Turkle (2015a) reviews some of the frustrations college faculty have trying to engage their students in the classroom. She discusses how students always want to feel connected online, so they disengage in class to check their e-mail, text their friends, or quickly scroll on social media.

She found that when students get bored or when a friend reaches out to them, they turn to their "circuit of apps" (p. 2) and the class cannot compete with their mobile devices. When a student is distracted, it interferes with the overall learning of the class. If students see another student texting, e-mailing, or shopping online in class, they may feel they have "permission" (p. 2) to mimic the same behavior.

In order to promote engagement, Turkle uses cell phone breaks so students can check their e-mail or text. Turkle also cites another instructor (Harvard Law School Professor Carol Steiker) who insists that no technology be present in class. She prefers for students to take handwritten notes, as opposed to typing notes on their laptops. Steiker felt that typed notes represent more of a transcription, rather than active engagement in processing the ideas in the notes. A transcription of the class resembles the behavior of a stenographer, rather than an engaged student (p. 6).

Ari Sherbill (2015) writes in his article "4 Effective Teaching Methods to WOW Your Students" that there are a few simple methods to use at the beginning of class to capture the attention of your students. If not done correctly, he states that you've lost your students completely. The first method he suggests is the "Desire Method." In order to best execute this method, he suggests writing a headline that best summarizes what will be addressed in class. The headline represents how students will benefit from the lesson. An example of a catchy headline could be, "the skills you learn this class will apply to all your other college classes." Polger emphasizes in his classes that the information literacy skills learned in class can be applied to students' lives (their work, family, personal, and professional life). The second method, "Feel the Pain," is when the teacher discusses the consequences of not adhering to the original headline/student benefit. An example of "feel the pain" could be discussing the reality of failing class if they do not listen in class or study for their midterms and final exams.

Sherbill's third teaching method to pique the curiosity of your students is to offer teasers of what they are going to learn. This involves previews and sneak peeks of future lessons and discussion topics. Finally, the fourth teaching method includes incorporating the VAK method of learning. The VAK method of learning focuses on visual, auditory, and kinesthetic learning materials that help promote learning. Incorporating visual tools such as YouTube videos, auditory materials such as live speeches, radio broadcasts, and podcasts, and kinesthetic tools like walking, running, and using the senses to learn (smelling, tasting) helps students learn more actively (Sherbill, 2015). This should remind the reader of Howard Gardner's theory of multiple intelligences in Chapter 1.

The Flipped Classroom

In "7 Things You Should Know about Flipped Classrooms" (Educause Learning Initiative, 2012), the author gives a "101" on flipped classrooms. In a traditional class, students come to class prepared to listen to an instructor give a lecture on a specific topic. Students are then to do homework on the topic they've just learned. In the flipped model, students watch prerecorded lectures before the class so that they come to class prepared to participate in hands-on activities. They may be required to complete a series of quizzes before coming to class to ensure that they have watched the video lectures.

This pedagogical method "flips" the typical lecture and homework elements. This means that the lecture is held before the class and the homework and other learning exercises are done in class. Flipped classrooms may promote student engagement, active learning, and experiential learning, but it does require that the students be self-motivated in their learning. It also assumes that students will take responsibility in their own learning and ensure that they will watch the videos and complete the quizzes before the class. It saves time if students are independent and disciplined and able to follow directions and take the initiative and spend the necessary time to prepare for class in advance.

In order for the flipped classroom to be successful, the student must take more personal responsibility in order to reap the benefits of this learning model. If done successfully, flipping the classroom promotes experiential learning and student engagement. It also saves time and allows for more interaction between the student and the instructor. For library instruction purposes, if students are consulting short instructional videos on how to use the library catalog or use a database, there might be more time for students to practice searching the databases with the librarian's assistance during the hands-on sessions (Arnold-Garza, 2014). The flipped classroom model works when librarians give tutorials, readings, and quizzes before the library instruction session and then the students come to class, prepared to practice what they've learned. The assumption is that the faculty member is on board and the students actually watch the videos and complete the readings before the library instruction session. If not, then they will be wasting their time. Moreover, the literature indicates that unless the instructor requires the student to do the work, or unless there is a grade associated with the flipped classroom model, the students won't do the work (Cohen, Lehner-Quam, Poggiali, & Wright, 2016; Stonebraker, 2015). For librarians to manage a flipped library instruction class, they must partner with classroom faculty to ensure that students watch the video tutorials or consult Blackboard so that they come prepared to the flipped classroom. It can be assumed that some review is necessary in the flipped classroom, so all learners are on the same wavelength. The flipped classroom is supposed to be an ideal way of getting much experiential learning, less lecturing, and increased engagement than the traditional model.

Students must be disciplined, self-directed, and eager to learn. If prerecorded videos represent half of the formula of a flipped classroom, then they must be engaging in order for the flipped classroom to work. In the next section, best practices for engaging video tutorials will be addressed.

There is a body of literature on using flipped classrooms for information literacy classes. Datig and Ruswick (2013), Rodriguez (2016), Wilcox Brooks (2014), and Cohen (2016) argue that flipped classrooms promote more active learning. They wanted to avoid "lecture fatigue" (Datig and Ruswick, 2013, p. 250) by having students watch video tutorials before the class. They gave four examples of learning activities that can be applied to the flipped classroom: searching databases, keyword searching, website evaluation, and identifying source types.

Kong (2014) argues that flipped classrooms frees up students' classroom time to interact with their peers and teachers, thereby maximizing their learning. Hands-on learning is done in class and the flipped classroom becomes learner-centered as opposed to teacher-centered (Kong, 2014, p. 161). Learner-centered classrooms are more engaging because the students are the focus, as opposed to focusing on what the teacher is saying. Kim, Kim, Khera, and Getman (2014) looked at how flipped classrooms can be designed effectively to foster learning and engagement. They discussed nine design principles in order for flipped classrooms to be successful. They are:

1. giving incentives for student preparation,
2. creating mechanisms to assess student understanding,
3. building adaptive feedback for individuals and groups,
4. providing enough time for students to complete tasks,
5. facilitating the building of a learning community,
6. inserting technology literacy,
7. providing opportunity to give students first exposure prior to class,
8. providing a clear connection between in-class and outside-class activities, and
9. providing structured guidance.

However, Strayer (2012) and Ash (2012) found that students' learning was not greatly affected by the flipped classroom versus the traditional classroom model of learning.

Video

To further engage students, video tutorials must be short, must meet the students' learning needs, must be tailored to a specific learning goal, and should contain an assessment tool (Blummer & Kritskaya, 2009; Bowles-Terry, Hensley, & Hinchliffe, 2010; Charnigo, 2009; Mestre, 2012; Tempelman-Kluit & Ehrenberg, 2003; Yang, 2009). Several studies debate the length of time for instructional videos. Some studies have recommended 6 minutes while some have cited no more than 3 minutes; while the latest studies have argued that 1- to 2-minute videos are most effective. The Library Minute hosted by Anali Perry (2014), librarian from Arizona State University Libraries, presents engaging video tutorials in 1 minute.

Currently there are 20 Library Minute videos and they promote library services and resources. Some videos are more instructional, while other videos promote library services and resources, but all are engaging. In order to be successful, video tutorials must be informal and casual, must target a specific set of learning outcomes, must not be overloaded with information, and must be selective in their goals. In order to avoid student boredom, library video tutorials should be broken into pieces and each piece should focus on a single goal. Having quizzes as part of the video tutorial also helps to improve engagement as students are asked to interact and participate in the video, as opposed to only watching it (Dixson, 2012).

Starting the Class

Lang (2016) argues that the first 5 minutes of teaching are the most important part of the class. The first 5 minutes offers an opportunity to capture students' attention, and if your introduction is not effective, then many students will not be engaged. Lang addresses four easy ways one can increase student engagement in the first 5 minutes of class. He discusses starting the class by (1) posing a question about the general theme of the lesson (i.e., what does note taking mean to you?), (2) reviewing the last class, (3) connecting their learning to other courses, and (4) giving appropriate time to take notes.

Learning Management Systems

Engaging students through the use of a learning management system can be an additional challenge. The advantage of having information literacy modules created for students to consult at their point of need (when they are conducting academic research) is very convenient. Librarians might find it a challenge to engage students in this online learning environment. However, requiring students to post discussion topics and responses and incorporating videos might improve engagement in the online environment (Chen, Lambert, & Guidry, 2010). In addition, having the online course instructor provide consistent and constant feedback also helps to move the course along. An online course must not be static but must be actively engaged with daily communications and interactions between faculty and student. Online teachers must use different techniques to engage their learners. Incorporating participatory modules such as blogs, commenting, discussion folders, live chats, and wikis may help with engagement (Brinthaupt, Fisher, Gardner, Raffo, & Woodard, 2011).

Repetition

Polger recounts that repetition can be an effective way to capture students' attention, especially ELLs (English language learners). Repetition is a strategy that some teachers use to emphasize important information. When using it, Polger reminds students that his use of repetition is on purpose as a reminder to study the material. This might provoke them to take down notes when the teacher repeats. Students then might become more actively aware of the teacher's use of repetition in future lessons. It is very important for the teacher to indicate that he/she is using repetition as a technique on purpose. Polger also uses repetition to emphasize the importance of a topic and to emphasize to students they should study it for their upcoming midterm or final exam. It serves as a "hint" for those students who are paying attention. Polger often uses repetition as a game (even though he is not fond of games), because after the midterm exam, he asks learners to refer to their notes to see if any of them noticed his repetitive notes were on the test. Polger uses repetition as a method to help students practice what they have learned by testing it multiple times in class.

Massive Open Online Courses

According to Turkle (2015a, p. 6), massive open online courses (MOOCs) are more engaging when they are coupled with face-to-face interaction. Her article suggests that even though students love being online, they prefer the structure of in-person interactions. Turkle's main argument is that MOOCs are convenient for learning but they do not promote student engagement (2015a, p. 8). The article emphasizes that engagement also occurs among other students and is not solely dependent on the instructor. MOOCs might be seen as lonely, anti-social, and unmotivating (Turkle, 2015a, p. 8).

Games

The more something feels like work, the less engaged students are (Vossler & Sheidlower, 2011). Conversely, the more something feels like play, the more engaged students will be. Sheidlower found this to be true when he created a low-tech game for a teacher's class assignment. The assignment was to teach students the difference between a politically liberal point of view and a politically conservative point of view in editorials. The reason for this was to allow students to locate and read conservative and liberal newspaper articles. After explaining what these points of view were, Sheidlower split the class in half and explained this game was for class "bragging rights!" He then had the classroom teacher keep score. Sheidlower had created multiple PowerPoint slides with each one having a fictitious newspaper headline, either conservative or liberal or neutral. An example of a neutral headline would be "Mayor Visits Flower Show." As each slide was shown, one headline per slide, anyone on either team could raise their hands and answer whether the headline was conservative or liberal or neutral and explain why they think so. Every correct answer earned that team one point. At the end of the game, the team with the most points won. The students really got into it and were fully engaged in the lesson. This could have been a higher tech game too if Sheidlower had used clickers. In that case, each individual student could have guessed, and at the end, the student with the highest score would have "won."

Questionnaire on Student Engagement in the Library Classroom

For Polger and Sheidlower's questionnaire on student engagement in the library classroom (QSELC), the last four questions report on how librarians assess how engaged their learners are by different methods. Following are some of the data culled from the last series of questions from our QSELC, which focus on practice, rather than on conceptual definition of student engagement.

For question #6, librarians reported on the various techniques they used to engage students during classes. Following are the eight most cited techniques used:

Technique	Percentage
Real-world examples	83
Class activities	80
Humor	79
Interaction	74
Instructional scaffolding	55
Body movements	51
Multimedia	42
Storytelling	30

For question #7, on the relationship between increased student engagement and learning, memory retention, and motivation, the replies are:

Increase in Student Engagement	Strongly Agree	Agree	Somewhat Agree
Improves learning	80%	19%	2%
Improves student retention	62%	30%	8%
Improved memory retention	59%	34%	7%
Improved motivation	57%	33%	9%
Improved student interest	61%	30%	9%

Most of the respondents commented that this question was flawed because it was "commonsense." Other responses focused on other factors (that instructors cannot control) that would affect student engagement. Other respondents commented that student engagement improves further with graduate-level students. Many reported that engagement is less challenging with graduate students rather than undergraduate learners. Polger would disagree with some of the respondents because it does depend on the academic discipline. As it will be discussed in Chapter 7, some graduate-level learners (in accounting) who have never been exposed to library instruction may present more challenges to the library instructor.

For question #8, librarians reported on their assessment techniques to measure students' level of engagement:

Assessment Measure	Percentage
Observational data such as feedback	72
In-class activities	63
Feedback forms	39
Surveys	27
Posttest	25
Formal in-person interviews	23
Pretest	14

For this particular question, 837 respondents completed this question and most (72%) cited observational data from faculty and students as their assessment measure.

For question #9, librarians were asked to evaluate the most effective engagement techniques. They were asked to score them as "very engaging," "somewhat engaging," "not very engaging," and "not engaging."

Engagement Technique	Very Engaging	Somewhat Engaging	Not Very Engaging
Hands-on time	76%	23%	1%
Real-world examples	50%	48%	2%
Multimedia	20%	64%	14%
Humor	38%	59%	3%
Storytelling	28%	57%	14%
Tailoring a handout	24%	56%	17%
Role-play	21%	52%	22%
Theatrics	6%	49%	37%
Clickers	11%	47%	32%

For the question #10 on factors that might affect student engagement, librarians were asked to reflect their own thoughts on what factors might influence the level of engagement. Librarians reported on the 10 most cited factors:

Factors That Might Affect Student Engagement	Percentage
Personality of instructor	81%
Disengaged faculty member	79%
Number of library instruction sessions a student has already taken	79%
Time of day	77%
Disruptive learners	66%
"One-shot" versus "embedded/credit courses"	65%
Level of the class	64%
Classroom space	63%
Technology	59%
Academic discipline	37%

A more in-depth discussion will be addressed in Chapter 6 that explores the various reasons learners might be disengaged in classes.

Interviews with Teaching Librarians

Over the course of four months, the authors recruited over 20 teaching librarians with Institutional Review Board (IRB) approval. They were asked more in-depth questions that related to what engagement means to them and what types of engagement techniques they use in their classes. The authors sought different librarians from diverse academic settings. The authors used convenience sampling by contacting colleagues whom they knew taught a variety of library instruction classes. The authors asked the following questions in their interviews:

1.   What does student engagement mean to you?
2.   What does student engagement look like in a library instruction class?
3.   What are some methods you have tried in order to engage your students?
4.   How do you measure how engaged your students are?

Linda Yau, former reference and instruction librarian at Bronx Community College, CUNY, believes that student engagement is an interest in learning as well as a curiosity for the topic of the workshop. Students would be serious in their learning, and value the importance of time. Students would be taking notes as to what the librarian said during the course, as well as during the activity portion of the workshop, and should be able to independently research on the instructed databases. Some methods she has tried are to show a short video clip, ask questions periodically throughout the lesson, and allow students to be able to explore their own on the instructed resources.

Post instruction, she hands out a short survey and reviews the answers. If the student answers all the questions correctly, she sees this as the student being pretty engaged. She continually makes minute adjustments to see if they have learned the appropriate subject of either the workshop or the information literacy course. After the course, students have approached her and reported a positive course grade.

Eamon Tewell, reference and instruction librarian at Long Island University, Brooklyn Campus, believes that student engagement means that students are meaningfully participating in their education, which can take place in their classes, in their personal life, or in campus life. One example that he thought exemplary was a student group that created a campus "dis-orientation" guide, which addressed the student debt crisis and the ways that banks and lenders capitalize on students' desire for an education, as well as resources for helping students adjust to university life and create positive social change both at the university and in the local community. These are students who are very much engaged in their education.

To him, student engagement in a library instruction class means that (1) students are actively participating in the classroom, and (2) they are getting something meaningful from the experience, whether personally (enjoyment, connections with other students) or intellectually (gaining new knowledge or understandings). Often student engagement in a library session looks like something as small as a flicker of a new understanding (that "light-bulb" moment that many educators live for), a robust conversation among a group of students working together, or students smiling while running back to the classroom after completing the last leg of a scavenger hunt. However small, these moments add up and ultimately contribute to a student's well-being personally or academically.

Lisa Ellis of Baruch College, CUNY, believes that student engagement is an opportunity facilitated by instructors where students are encouraged to participate to apply knowledge learned or explore new knowledge to learn. Instructors facilitate student engagement where students participate, either individually or in small groups, in some kind of class activity or respond to a question on a topic being explored. Lisa has demonstrated search techniques in her course-related lectures such as using proximity operators in full-text databases like Factiva or LexisNexis. She works through a problem, step-by-step, thinking aloud with each step. Then, she works through another example getting members of the class to participate with each step. She then posts an example for class members to try on their own while she walks around to see how each student is doing and help those having difficulty progressing through the problem. This is also where she may emphasize key points in the approach or other considerations to the class based on what kinds of problems a student may encounter. In the end, she works on a sample search topic as a group and works through the problem from beginning to end. Another method she has used to encourage student engagement is to conduct a poll and make use of clicker technologies where students are asked to respond to a question by selecting from the choices listed. She obtains a tally of the responses, and she reveals the true answer, and then, as a class, she reviews explanations for the reasons/factors that may attribute to the correct answer.

Student engagement is usually associated with student participation and interest in the lesson. It also relates to a vested interest or care about the outcome. It is sometimes advised to start student engagement with a class by working in small group activities to build student confidence where students are less likely to be self-conscious and reluctant to respond since there is safety in numbers where they can benefit by working together as a group to respond.

Pamela Pollack, former information literacy instructor at ASA College and children's nonfiction author, explains that engagement relates to how much the instructors care about their class and students, and vice versa. If you are not engaged with the students, you're at best giving them information they don't care about and can't relate to and ultimately it does not matter to them. It's the number one way you can determine whether you're being successful. If they're engaged, they're interested in what you're saying. Pam believes if they are looking at you, not looking at each other, then they are engaged. If they're sitting up, and not slumped back in their chair, then they are more engaged. If they're talking about the theme of the class, not chatting with other students, then she perceives her students to be engaged in the class.

Pam has tried teaching about fair sources and information and bias by bringing the three competing New York newspapers to class, giving one of each to each group and having them look at the same one or two stories with three different interpretations. She has had the students look for things that should be there but aren't, or asked them to find things that are just made up (like the stories about weapons of mass destruction in Iraq). Pam states that in 2015, Donald Trump gave examples of every kind of bias that she could talk about. She has had students read articles and have them put things in their own words. These are all ways to jumpstart the lesson that you're teaching. The students often said her class was their favorite of the term.

Pam uses students' level of participation to assess how engaged they are. If they're focused on the topic and have things to say and listen to others, then she knows they're engaged.

Nancy Falciani-White (Wheaton College) believes that student engagement represents the extent to which students' attention and/or thinking are focused on the task at hand.

In a library instruction class, student engagement might include:

- critically listening to or watching presented/lectured content;
- thinking about the research project, topic, question, search terms, etc.;
- searching for, evaluating, or reading information resources related to a presentation or their project;
- collaborating or discussing with classmates; and
- asking questions.

Some methods Nancy has tried in order to engage her students include the following:

- Only give instruction when students have a specific assignment that requires library resources, and ideally only after a topic is selected.
- Limit presentation/lecture time to 7- to 8-minute chunks, broken up with activities, videos, and so on.
- Make presentation/lecture, examples, activities, and the like relevant to the topic of the class and as relevant to students' research topics as possible. Try to ensure that a part of every class is dedicated to student research for their projects and tell them to make the most of it while both their professor and the librarian are there to help.
- Use active learning techniques (e.g., think–pair–share, round robin) where possible and appropriate.
- Have students do a presession assignment in which they answer questions about their topic/assignment, and have a space to ask any other questions about their research specifically or the library more generally. Use these responses to guide the face-to-face class session, making students aware when the content is in response to one of their classmates' questions.

For presession assignments, she can tell how engaged students are by the quality and depth of their answers. In-class, she usually evaluates their engagement through observation or by the questions they ask. She walks around the classroom a lot when she is teaching and so is able to see at least if students are on-task on their computers. During active learning activities, students are expected to either volunteer or be called on, so it quickly becomes obvious if they are engaged or not.

Dr. Shelley Blundell feels that student engagement means more than engaging the students in the learning experience—it means making the students an integral part of their own learning experiences, and working with them to develop the self-confidence (and eventually, the autonomy) to be integral to the design and facilitation of their learning experiences, so that their engagement is as intrinsic and authentic as possible.

A library instruction class that creates a rich student engagement environment must be proactive, interactive, and reactive. To be proactive, the librarian should work with the instructor prior to the instruction itself to design an experience that is contextual to the needs of the course and the students, and that imparts the most critical information in a dynamic and responsive way.

To be interactive, the instruction must draw on student commentary and insights throughout the library instruction session, and allow students to contribute to the instruction session from start to finish—this can include allowing students to provide input on learning objectives they believe should be covered during the session, and giving them autonomy in determining how they will demonstrate their achievement of learning outcomes after the session concludes. To be reactive, the librarian must pay attention to the needs of the instructor and the students before the session, during the session, and after the session, and react accordingly. This includes "changing direction" during the instruction session if necessary, and providing students with the opportunity to do midpoint "muddy point" analysis, so that the librarian can "react" to whether or not the session is actually imparting the knowledge it set out to impart.

In addition to asserting the willingness of the librarian to be a collaborative partner to the instructor (perhaps encouraging further interaction and collaboration), such a strategy encourages authentic student engagement by making them an integral part of their learning experience, and allowing them to work with and learn from their peers as they work with and learn from the librarian.

She uses many methods to engage students, depending on the needs of the students and the instructor, but here are the top three methods she strongly recommends others investigate and incorporate, based on the success she has had with these methods:

For students who are new to college (freshmen and the like, no matter their age), she strongly recommends using the question formulation technique prior to conducting any library instruction. This technique works best if the prompt given is contextually related to the course in which the library instruction takes place, and serves as an excellent critical thinking stimulation exercise, prior to discussing information literacy or various academic research tactics they will need in higher education.

From learning objectives and outcomes, to evaluation results, to lesson plans and course instructor expectations, sharing with students why you are doing what you're doing, and not just expecting them to take your word for it that what you're imparting in the library instruction session is crucial to their learning experience, engages them on a level they are not typically used to, and therefore makes them a part of their learning experience. She has found student engagement to be much richer (and that more students are inclined to participate in a library instruction session) when she makes her session as transparent as possible, and allows the students to see where each piece/part of the session fits in with their learning in the course, and beyond.

She suggests that librarians should pay attention to social cues in class and give students the opportunity to ask questions and contribute to discussions. She recommends using assessment such as multiple-choice and open-ended questions, both of which can be answered anonymously, which allows students the opportunity to authentically express their opinions related to their levels of engagement. Furthermore, the responses allow her to improve on future instruction, as well, by reacting to student suggestions and incorporating said suggestions into future courses.

Dr. Naomi Gold, a freelance information literacy trainer, explains that in the context of library instruction, student engagement means that most or all students in a library instruction session are actively interested in and understand the relevance of library instruction for their academic progress. That sense of the relevance of instruction for their progress may be targeted to their work and assignments for one particular class, as is often the case when a professor brings a specific class into the library for instruction about research for that class. The sense of relevance may also be general, although often it is not. That is, in her experience when a library instruction session is conducted along the lines of a general introduction to the library, students' attention, receptiveness, and retention are usually low.

In her experience, perception of student engagement is best described as a sense of the students' energy. When students are apathetic and uninterested, this is often visible by their facial expressions and the quality (or lack thereof) of their eye contact. When students are engaged, the quality of their eye contact, body language, and the energy they "give back" to the librarian are palpable. In addition, the presence or absence of comments and questions are a strong indicator of the level of student engagement in a library instruction session.

Through the process of engaging in library instruction at four different institutions, she learned very viscerally that presenter and "audience" are engaged in an exchange of energy. Much like an actor, she learned to "feel" the energy and interest of her various classes. Any actor will tell about the reality of this exchange of energy and sense he/she has developed about specific types of audiences. Teaching has much of the same dynamic.

The most successful method she has used is reinforcing with the particular professor who has scheduled the instruction session that the students *must* have a specific assignment with which they are dealing, and that is, for lack of a better term, "in their faces." She uses the students' concrete immediate need to deal with a specific assignment as a jumping-off point for the instruction, and verbally reassures the students at the start of the session that they will be leaving with skills and materials (e.g., specific articles and books) that will be relevant for that assignment.

It has been her consistent experience that student attention and retention in library instruction sessions are enormously enhanced when that instruction is coupled with an immediate, concrete need. In fact, she would go so far as to say that this component (or the lack thereof) can make or break a library instruction session.

Along these same lines, she always asks students in the course of the session to volunteer to tell the class the subject with which they're working, so that she can demonstrate library website features and research techniques using the specific topic of a specific student.

Prior to this, she asks the course professor for a list of prospective topics on which his/her students are working, so that she can also prepare some ready-made, "canned" searches for the purposes of demonstration.

Measurements are often subjective, that is, she gauges the level of student engagement based on factors such as the liveliness of the class, eye contact, and discussion. The subsequent comments from professors in follow-up e-mail are often a satisfying, anecdotal, though not *quantitative* way of gauging how engaged students were. Finally, it has not been unusual for her to receive e-mail from students either asking further questions or letting her know that a session has been helpful, that he or she feels much more confident about library research, and/or that he or she has completed an assignment successfully.

She is convinced (as are many librarians engaged in instruction) that one of the most effective means of enhancing and perhaps even ensuring student engagement is to put into place a campus-and-curriculum-wide program that integrates the library into curricular activities with the same rigor as, for example, those respective institutions' core courses. This would require three things: (1) institution-wide commitment to integration of library instruction in this way; (2) at least one mandatory, credit-bearing library instruction course; and (3) sufficient library faculty to conduct all of the new courses and instruction sessions that will result.

Dr. Maura Smale, chief librarian at New York City College of Technology, CUNY, believes that student engagement is about students participating as fully as they can in their college experience. She believes that students are engaged when they participate in the class in most (if not all) ways: they come to class, they contribute to discussion, they do the reading (if there's reading), and they stay on task with what's happening in the class. She uses classroom games and quizzes to encourage students to do the reading. Typically, she asks brief questions at the end of a class like "What one thing did you learn today that you didn't know previously?" Anecdotally, she takes note of how each class goes as compared to other classes she has taught, and tries to make adjustments accordingly.

Daniel Payne, head of instruction at OCAD University (Toronto, Ontario, Canada), argues that when one hears of student engagement in an academic context, one invariably thinks of the National Survey of Student Engagement (NSSE). Although he is slightly distrustful of such quantitative attempts to measure something so essentially unmeasurable as "engagement," the approximately 100 NSSE questions do begin to unpack this measurement benchmark in a way that not only allows students' concerns to be heard with clarity, but also reflects their values, goals, and aspirations in postsecondary education.

In Canada, the university that has consistently topped the rankings for the past five years is Canada's first private, nonprofit liberal arts school Quest University (and Mr. Payne notes that he is responding from a mid-sized, publicly funded art and design university). Perhaps tellingly, the school has only participated in the survey for five years! Despite potential skewed results based on the "private status" (most universities in Canada are publicly funded) and most definitely its small size, *Maclean's Magazine* reports that "in the five years it has participated in NSSE, Quest has come out at the top four times, and second once, when students rated their entire educational experience." The categories of evaluation include higher-order learning, quantitative reasoning, collaborative learning, student–faculty interaction, effective teaching practices, and supportive environment. The resounding top ranking in all six major statistical categories implies that something is indeed propelling the unbelievably high ratings for student engagement. What is Quest University's "secret to success"? What aspect of the curriculum can foster this ubiquitously successful record?

The course work is innovatively structured so that students attend a rigorous two-year foundation program that introduces students to broad fields across the arts and sciences, one that is rooted in the classical educational principles of rhetoric, ethics, and logic—the scientific method. Exploring various modes of writing is firmly integrated in the curriculum to ensure that students can effectively and emotively convey their ideas through text-based communication. Following this, students meet with instructors to propose a major senior thesis project, then spend the ensuing two years developing their own personalized course work based on the requirements of their individualized research projects. The students, in essence, create their own curriculum under the close mentorship guidance of faculty. In addition, all students "engage in experiential learning off-campus," which includes "opportunities for field work, study abroad, and internships."

Payne believes that it tangibly demonstrates that the majority of students want a rigorous understanding of core topics, subjects, theories, or concepts that have been developed throughout our human history but more importantly, that they want to be trusted to engage independently with these core competencies on their own terms, tailored to meet the specificities of their own skill sets. Certainly the ongoing mentorship of their peers is essential; however, at Quest University—because students are setting curriculum by deciding the courses needed and how they should be conveyed—the teaching faculty would be included in a student's peer group.

In short, students want to learn how to learn in collaboration with their peers rather than to be solely taught how to learn by rote in a "top-down" hierarchical model (in colloquial design terminology: instead of a peer-mentorship model of education, it is a "master-mystery" one!). The distinction is not always clearly identifiable, but the essence is that students will be able—definitely with guidance and instruction—to define their own course of inquiry rather than have it forced on them based on tradition, convenience, or sheer lethargy on the part of administrators or teaching faculty.

In an information literacy session at any postsecondary institution, the learning outcomes should embody the above ethos where instructors foster a library "ecology" in order to help students begin the research process. The students' input is as crucial as that of the professional knowledge of a librarian; thus Brenda Dervin's "sense-making" model becomes the ideal forum with which to engage in student-centered curricular design.

In a way, the library—through its services and collections—acts as a foil to the set rigidity of the curriculum. It offers a multitude of access points, opportunities for exploration, and sites for fortuitous encounters with information that can empower students to contrast, critique, modify, and even contradict the formalism of textbooks and the curriculum as a whole. So an ideal information literacy session makes students aware of this power, but encourages them to use it wisely, in that they need to be able to *make sense* of the vastly complex array of resources available through a library collection. In essence, a librarian should serve as a way-finding consultant for students, helping them learn to navigate information systems on their own terms and create personalized searching models that will serve them well in future research endeavors.

This is particularly important for Daniel, given that he works in an art and design–based university environment. The intricacies of the creative process are well-studied scientifically; but in real life, such research oftentimes generates more questions and creates greater uncertainty and doubt than it does in answering questions or proving facts! Thus students at his school have the doubly confusing responsibility of making sense of academic research as well as mastering the processes required for creative production.

So the ideal information literacy session challenges students profoundly and perhaps even makes them feel a little lost! Yet, critically, a message must be conveyed that getting lost can be good—especially for creative research purposes—and that some of the most divergent, interdisciplinary ideas can emerge from this sense of chaos. But ultimately we need to provide wayfinding abilities to help students find their pathway through the complexities of our new information environment; when librarians help them learn mastery over academic information networks, students can begin incorporating these domains into their own personal sense-making cognitive models.

Because he teaches in an art and design–based university, in creating information literacy sessions or offering reference services, it is important to use metaphors and analogies that are rooted in studio-based learning models. He tries to find commonalities between both scholastic and creative processes, so that students may ultimately use their "academic" research skills fluidly in support of their creative work in the studio.

A powerful tool for more standardized information literacy—especially within the liberal arts and science courses—is to offer metaphors or analogies between creative research processes and information literacy.

- By advocating for using broad reference resources at the beginning of one's research to achieve an expansive knowledge of current research on a topic, and then encourage student to use more focused information sources as they work their way through the research process, Daniel urges students to begin a process of moving from core art and design encyclopedias to monographs or exhibition catalogues and to the fine-tuned granularity of a peer-reviewed journal article. This same process is oftentimes used by students who sit in front of an easel preparing to create a painting: one begins with preparatory sketches from source images, then maps out broad forms in a painting using larger brush strokes, and then gradually layers fine details on the canvas using smaller grade brushes.

- In helping students to think about structuring their research-based ideas to build arguments, Daniel encourages them to consider conclusions or theories from academic research literatures as individual forms that could be arranged on a canvas; some core ideas—central to one's research thesis—should be placed in the foreground; other secondary ones are moved to the background.

- In teaching research methodologies or in showing how library research can enact the learning outcomes of a course, he always uses mnemonic images/symbols to represent the concepts. For example, in discussing deductive research—where one works from broad theories to analyze specific case studies—he uses an inverted pyramid shape, and then adds text boxes on it indicating the research tools one would use to enact deductive reasoning. For inductive inquiry, he uses the same inverted pyramid, but always starts with the case study at the bottom of the symbol, then works his way up to the widest part of the triangular image, based on the premise that inductive research takes specific case studies and builds broader theories from these particular examples.

- And along these lines of inquiry, he always encourages students to conceptualize academic theories as one of the "mediums" that they can use in their artistic work. Just as a painting students knows how to stretch a canvas, prime it, mix paint colors, and then use specific paintbrushes or palette knives to layer paint on their canvases, so aesthetic ideas become one of the "pigments" that can be added to the overall painting of research to inform its artistic message to viewers.

- Instruction on library search tools should be conducted much as an instructor teaches in the studio: he/she models for students how to use a certain artistic technique once, then the students take it and "make it their own"; they use the technique to explore and find their own voice through their medium, which will change according to the student's creative goals in executing an artwork. He hopes to do the same, whether it's searching a library catalogue, a discovery layer, or a subject-specific database. Decisions on how and when to use these resources will, hopefully, change according to what sort of research, calculation, or writing a student is conducting.

- He conceptually engages students by showing a step-by-step guide on how to use a database. He tries to show what conceptually engaging articles, and by consequence, ideas can be retrieved through a research tool. By focusing on the end results—not so much on the technical specificities of the process—students are inspired to find out how to retrieve similar research-based knowledge on their own. When art students are shown an iconic work of art, they are conceptually engaged through critical viewing; then they immediately go to the studio to see how they can use their own technical skill sets to model, emulate, or incorporate elements of the artwork into their own creations. Students first attend an information literacy session on libraries, their histories, the processes used to organize information, and current issues challenging educational institutions. Second, the students must pick themes from the discussion, and then propose an installation for the library space. Through a process of negotiation—between student, faculty member, and librarian—a work is eventually approved, displayed, and critiqued in the library. This latter process, a form of peer-review essential to all studio-based learning models, is a critical moment to dialogically establish the aesthetic and conceptual merits of a work. Through these interactions with the practices of studio-based learning, creative research learning models are emulated in the library's information literacy program.

> One of the most dynamic aspects of art is its open and essentially ambiguous ability to transmit ideas that cannot rely on the specificity of text-based or verbal modes of communication; so for visual learners, these sorts of intangible dialogues are a most invaluable tool for starting a chain reaction of ideas, an essential ingredient for creativity.

As the information literacy program is not officially linked to the curriculum, it is difficult to measure the impact on engagement in a quantitative manner. Extensive qualitative feedback from both instructors and students is used to help direct the flow of instruction sessions; this feedback will be gleaned from informal surveys, focus group discussion, and the like. Faculty input is of particular importance for librarians, as they are the key stakeholders who allow access to their courses, imbed instruction sessions into the syllabus and, occasionally, structure assignments that are informed by information literacy outcomes.

The e-resources librarian does keep rigorous tabulations of database statistics, and it is always interesting to theorize how spikes in usage are possibly a response to information literacy instruction. For example, in presentations to first year visual and material culture courses (VISC 1001: beginnings to 1800; VISC 1002: 1800 to the present), the librarian will be able to offer an introduction to library research to all first year students. In the seminar for this survey course, the Johns Hopkins journal collection, *Project Muse* is prominently highlighted,; somewhat consistently for the past few years in the analysis of database usage, there have been noted an inordinately high number of access counts, page views, and downloads for this particular database in relation to other collections, for example, Sage Journals, Cambridge or Oxford Journals Online, Wiley, or Taylor & Francis. But such hypothetical correlations would be difficult, if not impossible, to ascertain.

Many scientists and researchers have effectively analyzed the characteristics of individual and group creativity; however, it is essentially futile to attempt to create a mathematical theorem to establish the exact formal characteristics of an artwork in order to ascertain whether or not it is of aesthetic merit. Efforts to quantify form, line, composition, and color palette in an attempt to scientifically calculate when an artist's work will be defined as a "work of art" are chimeras; these artistic formulae evade measurement and, perhaps, should even be specifically removed from scientific measurement! Artistic quality cannot simply be codified through a quantitative measurement of specific formal elements, but, instead, comprises a somewhat subjective mix of personal tastes, market-driven values, current events, and aesthetic traditions; in addition, these values are constantly shifting as the art world constantly seeks new forms, mediums, and consequent messages to promote and elevate. Likewise, library support for nascent creative researchers must rely on somewhat "unmeasurable" elements in order to maintain relevancy and utility in assisting art and design students to engage with and make sense of their worlds.

Mariana Regalado (Brooklyn College, CUNY) feels that student engagement means students see value in the learning endeavor. She thinks students are engaged when they get excited about the research process as well as getting what they need for the next step. She starts instruction sessions (all one-shots) by asking students what research is and what steps they take when they do it (not necessarily academic research)—it's been pretty successful because it helps them to see that they already know about research, and it helps frame the academic library instruction session as new skills for the tool kit. Also, always, always, always, hands-on library lecturing is boring! She measures how engaged students are, by participation mostly; are they doing research during the class or are they asking questions?

Kelly Hamilton, a new librarian and trained ESL teacher in New York City, states that student engagement means the learner is using all of his or her skills to learn something and is in sync with what the teacher is sharing with the class. During library instruction, student engagement is evident when the learner is eager to follow the direction of the instructor and is able to successfully work individually or in small groups. She thinks that differentiation is a good way to reach students and not only keep them interested but also enable them to successfully absorb information and successfully duplicate the lesson when using the library or doing research. Success is measured by duplication, through critical thinking, creativity, and ideas for how to move forward armed with new ideas.

Alexandra Deluise (instruction coordinator at Queens College, CUNY) believes that student engagement is accomplished when she inspires students to become independent users of library resources by navigating through the information highway. Students are engaged when they're listening, they are not on their electronic devices, they're in the moment, and they're asking relevant questions and simultaneously trying out their skills on the computer. She looks at each student before beginning. She gets their attention before starting the presentation. She varies her voice and tries to speak clearly. She asks questions and calls on students. She brings personal experience as it might help in understanding a concept or idea. She tries to use humor. She shows a few short video clips on the research process instead of explaining everything herself. She tries to engage the professor as well, because an engaged professor is the best ally.

The professor will support and underscore concepts that she is conveying. If she feels she is losing the students or they're bored, she will use the microphone or stop talking and take a pause. If the class is quiet, she stops and asks them why. Calling on a student to come to the trainer's station and explain an idea to the other students helps too. She brings in techniques she learned in a mini course taken from Queens College faculty entitled "Using Theatre Techniques in Teaching," taught by a drama professor. In the course, Alexandra learned about presence, pitch, breathing, and classroom setup, and so on.

If students are both listening and asking relevant questions, then she knows she is on the right track. If they thank her, then she knows they at least paid some attention. If they seem more comfortable with their research at the end than when they first sat down, she knows something clicked. If she had talked about activating their IDs at the borrowing desk after class and she later sees them there lined up, then she knows they were listening. While she knows she will not engage every student, she tries to be the best instructor possible and be up on her game, with a workable and prepared lesson and a pleasant classroom environment.

Steven Ovadia (acting chief librarian, LaGuardia Community College, CUNY) thinks that student engagement involves two things:

1. the act of keeping students interested in their education, helping them to connect with their college, but also helping them to move along, semester by semester, until they graduate; and

2. the act of keeping students interested in learning at the classroom level.

These are hands-on activities that put students in control of some of their learning. It's what allows students to immediately practice and demonstrate what they've learned. Student engagement means hands-on work where students aren't just learning, but are practicing them. In terms of the one-shot library classes, Steve tries to facilitate conversations and give students time to work on their own things while he walks around. The success and implementation varies from class to class. In terms of the credit classes, it's a little bit easier to put students into groups and to create longer-form projects designed to get students working on their own. In those situations, engagement might have them identifying what makes a scholarly article scholarly, based on hard copies from different journals, or having students work with databases and then report out on their findings. He measures engagement by the energy level in the class. If students are focused on the task, they're engaged. If the energy is low and they seem disinterested in what they're doing (heavy eyes, phones out, talking about anything but the task at hand), the engagement is low.

John Drobnicki (reference librarian at York College, CUNY) writes that it's more than just "class participation" or "paying attention." He believes that it means that students see that there is a connection between what is being covered in the class and what their personal specific information need is, and therefore come to the realization that the information literacy session is worth their time. Again, it's more than just "class participation" or "paying attention." When students are engaged, they're actively listening, asking questions about what was said by the instructor, and perhaps more importantly asking questions about what was *not* covered by the instructor, because they see that there is or should be an application of the knowledge that the instructor did not foresee. He tries to pique their interest by telling them how he is going to show them things that will not only help with the specific class that the information literacy session is linked to, but also help them in *all* of their classes at York. He walks around. He asks questions and encourages students to ask questions. He uses humor as needed to establish a rapport with them.. As he walks around, he constantly tries to make eye contact and see if students are not only paying attention, but also understanding what is being presented based on facial expressions, or if they're not on the same page (both literally and figuratively). Obviously, in a one-shot class, not every student is going to be engaged, and the instructor has to have a balance between those who "get it" and those who have no interest in "getting it." That's the ongoing challenge.

Dan Sich (research and instructional services librarian, University of Western Ontario, London, Ontario, Canada) believes engagement is about getting students listening, participating, answering questions, and asking questions. He feels that they are engaged if they are participating, asking and answering questions, giving good eye contact. He uses different methods such as asking a lot of questions, hands-on exercises, group and individual exercises, graded assignments, student presentations during "class." He measures how engaged they are by having a postsession "3 minutes, 3 questions" and by analyzing the frequency of students' responses, questions, eye contact, quality of students' assignments, and quality/depth of students' presentations. Most of his assessment techniques are formative. The assignments and postsession "3 minutes, 3 questions" are summative.

Karen Okamoto (reference and interlibrary loan librarian, John Jay College of Criminal Justice, CUNY) feels that engagement means being student-centered, flexible, and responsive by using teaching methods that can be hands-on, collaborative, iterative, experiential, and creative. It means students being interested in learning and applying their knowledge and experiences to the course material. She can identify if her students are engaged by their level of participation in discussions, if students ask questions, students' aha moments, and students doing rather than listening (i.e., students being active learners). Karen uses group exercises and discussions, group presentations, scavenger hunts both online and in the physical library, using student research topics, and she uses clickers. In order to measure success, she uses end-of-class surveys for student feedback, but her methods have been informal, for example, the number of students who follow the class, ask questions, and complete assignments; and informal feedback from teaching faculty.

Robin O'Hanlon (public services manager, Levy Library, Icahn School of Medicine, Mount Sinai School of Medicine, New York City) feels that an engaged student is a student who is actively learning. She thinks it goes beyond just paying attention. An engaged student is really taking in what the instructor is saying and trying to apply it to his or her own research or education. O'Hanlon keeps students engaged during library instruction, which can be tough for a number of reasons. One, there's usually a lot of content to go over in a short amount of time. Two, the content is usually brand new to the students, so they can feel overwhelmed. Three, students may have difficulty connecting the content to their real lives. She thinks a lot of students walk in with that classic misconception of "What do I need the library for when everything is on the Internet?" This isn't always the case, but it's common. So before you can even start teaching, you have to really consider these barriers to engagement. If you can get over those hurdles, O'Hanlon thinks student engagement can present itself in a number of ways. Participation is usually a good sign of student engagement. If students are asking questions, especially about concepts they're learning about for the first time, that's a great sign. If a student is taking notes, that's another good sign. She tries to make instruction sessions as interactive as possible. She uses timed group activities a lot, as it gets students thinking, but the time limit keeps them focused. It can be as simple as getting students into a group and asking them to come up with keywords. O'Hanlon also always uses a student volunteer if demonstrating a database. She also uses activities and exercises throughout the session, rather than all the way at the end. She also uses interactive polls during presentations—these are really fun and keep students interested. More generally, she tries to keep content interesting and relevant. For a lot of students, information about the library can be dry, so try to make it relatable. If doing an instruction session for a specific class, always reach out to the faculty member in advance and try to get him or her to share information on what the class is working on. Then incorporate this content into the class. She also experiments with using games—these can be fun, but they do eat up a lot of time. She believes the struggle for many librarians (in the classroom) is time. Often, there is only an hour orientation session to meet with students. The time restriction creates this tremendous pressure to show students how to do everything and give them tons of information! But this is impossible and overwhelms the students. She measures engagement, the old fashioned way—observation. Sometimes you can tell just by looking at someone if they're really engaged or not. If someone looks bored or is literally falling asleep, he or she is obviously not engaged. If students aren't reacting to anything you're saying, they're not engaged. If they're not asking questions, they're probably not engaged. Beyond that, she's also tried pre- and posttesting to test students' knowledge before and after the instruction session. She also does follow-up surveys and always includes a "how interesting was this session to you?" type question.

Toni Ann Kaminski, former information literacy instructor at ASA College, explains that student engagement means much more than just communicating information to students. Toni Ann feels that her students need to teach her as much as she teaches them. The classroom is a space for interaction between individuals, and everyone should feel comfortable enough to take part. If she goes into class and her students have transformed her lesson past her expectations, then that means they are fully engaged. Student engagement happens when they get past their preconceived notions of a library. She reminds students that the library has transformed from just a room or building, into an electronic component available any time of day. Students really enjoy the opportunity to exercise their detective capabilities, so she often creates activities based upon that belief. Kaminski incorporates discussion, group work, and activities on a daily basis. She tries to make sure that anything related to library tasks are computer based and interactive. She knows her class is engaged by how awake and responsive they are. If her expectation is to have at least 1–2 responses and 6–10 students respond, then she has found success. If students who usually don't participate take the time to say something, then that is an indicator of success. Toni Ann comments that it has become more difficult to captivate an audience when you are competing against technology. She attempts to form the connection between a library class and all other classes that they will be taking. It is not an easy task, but it becomes a much more rewarding one.

Michael Kahn, learning commons librarian at the Brooklyn Campus of the College of New Rochelle, explains that student engagement is when students pay attention and find the lesson interesting and relevant. Engagement happens when they actively contribute to the creation of knowledge as it relates to the subject being taught. When students ask questions and answer questions that are on topic and are thinking in a manner that is provocative and innovative, they are engaged. Kahn begins his lessons by activating prior knowledge, and establishing why students should be interested in the lesson ("what's in it for them"). He allows students who are hesitant to speak in class because of their limited English language skills or a fear of being wrong to write responses in their notebooks. He then circles the class and checks on what they are writing, offering praise and constructive criticism. By building up students' confidence, he encourages students to then share their answers with the class. Michael reads students' responses in their notebooks. He also has students work on worksheets in pairs, which he will collect. He will have students complete lab work searching for sources in databases or evaluating websites and evaluate their work.

Elaine M. Provenzano, marketing and assessment librarian at Manhattanville College, Purchase, New York, teaches one-shots and credit-bearing information literacy classes. She writes that students are engaged when they are actively immersed in their work, whether it is reading and reflection, topic selection, research, or working independently. Students take interest, ask questions, and readily offer input to class discussion and group work. Although students each have unique learning styles, the degree to which they interact with each other, their instructor, and course content will have the most positive outcome. Student engagement differs depending on the type of library instruction class. The key is to know your audience:

- One-shot workshop

  - Personalize—Assess the needs of the class with the professor, beginning with a review of the syllabus and class requirements.
    - Where are they currently in their research?
    - "Is there anything that you would particularly like me to focus on, i.e., finding secondary sources, citation, annotated bibliography, working with primary sources?" This allows her to customize a program that will more readily meet the students where they are.
  - In the classroom, immediately engage students by making introductions and asking about their major and areas of interest.

Before the class, survey what their learning expectations for the workshop are. At the end of the class, survey what is still puzzling them. This helps them not only to define areas where they still need help but also to fine-tune future instruction content.

- First year students

  - There are a series of one-shot classes throughout their first year, beginning with an introduction to the library during the first few weeks of the fall semester, and several as they begin their writing assignments. The same methods of engagement as mentioned previously would also apply, as far as developing a personal rapport with students. "What do you want from your college library? What did you learn today that you did not know before? What do you still want to know more about?"

  - As this tends to be a restless group, the first meeting involves an activity—the library scavenger hunt. After brief introductions, students are divided into four or five groups and given a picture of a library space, for example, the reference desk. Each group finds its location, writes a description of the space, why it is beneficial, and how students could they see themselves using it. The groups then take turns describing the space to each other. This is a fun exercise that gets students to explore the whole library building sans a monotonous tour. Students become more interested in learning about the library when hearing a "review" from their peers and being actively involved in the teaching.

  - In the spring, there are two library instructional visits to assist first year students with the freshman essay. The "Introduction to Research" class is focused on developing a research question for their topic. Using a concept map, students learn how to brainstorm their topic, which helps them in creating keyword search strategies. After a review of scholarly versus popular articles, students use the CRAAP test rubric to evaluate their own sources. This personalized approach to reviewing their own selections makes any distinctions more apparent. Then move on to discuss how to create an annotated bibliography, and they begin to understand why they need to validate their citations, and if the citations are appropriate for their paper. The follow-up workshop is held a few weeks into their research to review search strategies, evaluation, and answer any other questions that have come up in the interim.

- One-credit learner information system class: Fundamentals of library research in the humanities

  - For a 10-session library instruction class, engagement with students is more complex, having time to engage more deeply with students in each area of instruction. As this is a one-credit class, content creation revolves around the final project, an annotated bibliography on a topic of their choice. The final project is worth 30 percent of their final grade. Therefore, each class session focuses on a different aspect of library research, beginning with an overview of academic honesty and plagiarism, topic development, search strategies, evaluation of sources in books, scholarly articles and websites, and MLA citation, culminating in an annotated bibliography that includes seven vetted sources.

Engagement methods she has used in her classes include the following:

Flipped classroom—Students are assigned reading and tutorials, which are completed outside of the classroom. After reviewing the materials on plagiarism and cite-*right* chapters on citation, they create two reflection journals in Blackboard, answering three questions: "What did you already know?"; "What did you not know?" and "What are you interested in knowing more about?" Not only are students more engaged in critical analysis, but also their answers help her assess where she needs to direct her efforts with instruction. She begins the following class with a brief discussion of their findings.

She likes the experience to be as personalized as possible, which is why students can choose any hypothetical question and topic within the humanities for the one-credit class, "Fundamentals of Library Research in the Humanities." When students are working on a topic of interest, they are more engaged in the process.

LOC hunt—To help students understand the Library of Congress classification system, she gives them an LOC bookmark and asks them to pick out their major/area of interest, for example, music. She then has them go to that area of the stacks and "browse," so they learn not only how material is organized but also how to use the collection.

When students are learning how to search the catalog to find reference materials, books, or journals, she gives them 10 minutes to locate the physical object, bring it back to the classroom, and explain why they chose it. She also explains how to use the table of contents and index to more easily identify if the material is useful for their research. Learning about the physical materials aids them to better identify and understand the materials when found in online eBooks and databases.

Students are broken up into groups and are given physical materials, that is, newspapers, trade magazines, journals, and popular magazines. Each group presents what type of material they have and how it could be used in their research.

Students conduct a CRAAP test on their sources and share the results with the class.

She measures her successes by asking students to create reflection journals, she evaluates their research questions, she analyzes their homework assignments, she looks at their midterm exam grades, she evaluates the success of their final research project, and she conducts library surveys and college surveys. Finally, she has ongoing communication with her students using e-mail, questions, and in-person meetings during office hours.

In this chapter, the authors, along with over 20 librarians, helped focus on what it means to be engaged and offered a variety of engagement strategies and methods. Chapter 5 explores how librarians can successfully engage learners outside the library classroom.

CHAPTER FIVE

Engaging beyond the Library Classroom

Teaching is not limited to the classroom.

—Sylvia Grider, 1995

This chapter focuses on the various physical and virtual spaces outside the library classroom where learning might take place. The library and its electronic resources contain many physical and virtual teaching spaces. Without a librarian being actively immersed in teaching, the classroom is just a stagnant and lifeless collection of computers and chairs.

Reference Desk

The reference desk provides an excellent location for learning to occur. Elmborg (2002) and Woodard (2005) argue that one-on-one teaching exists at the reference desk and beyond the classroom. Elmborg writes, "the reference desk can be a powerful teaching station—more powerful, perhaps, than the classroom" (2002, p. 455). Learning is best accomplished with dialogue, with interaction, and by using different teaching methods (Adler, 2013).

At Polger's institution, the reference desk workstation contains two monitors, one for the librarian and the other for the learner. The learner can follow the librarian using the learner monitor while sitting down on a stool. This may lead to the learners asking more questions and remaining at the reference desk for a longer period of time. It also could lead to repeat visits, more in-depth learning such as research consultations, and a longer reference interview (Banks & Pracht, 2008; Beck & Turner, 2001; Carlson, 2007; Desai & Graves, 2008; Elmborg, 2002; Ferguson & Bunge, 1997; Mardikian & Kesselman, 1995; Rader, 1980; Roy & Hensley, 2016; Tyckoson, 2001; Woodard, 2005). Successful teaching techniques at the desk could include implementing the reference interview, asking open-ended questions, active listening, fostering a dialogue, and taking advantage of any teachable moments by selecting appropriate information to teach (Adler, 2013; Coonin & Levine, 2013).

Online/Massive Open Online Courses

One of the main differences in how we teach online versus face-to-face is the lack of immediate engagement in the online environment. It is a challenge for librarians teaching online because we do not see our learners' facial expressions, there is no observable body language, and there is no interaction between learners and the rest of the class. Obviously, they also do not see us and our facial expressions and body language, or hear our vocal inflections. Therefore, learners must be self-directed, motivated, and independent. Unlike the traditional class, which is scheduled and therefore provides a framework for the learner, online class requires students to be more disciplined in order to learn with success. The traditional class provides a setting where learners acquire knowledge from each other through various interactions, in addition to learning from the instructor. In a Web-based environment, learning can be asynchronous and isolated. In order to improve engagement in Web-based instruction, content should be delivered in small spurts (content spread over many Web pages as opposed to being solely placed on one large Web page), incorporated in images and video content, and the librarian should ensure that the text is concise. Encouraging interaction and participation by having discussion board topics and requiring learners to post topics and respond to topics might improve engagement. Adding synchronous learning opportunities, such as Google hangouts, GoToMeetings, or Skype chats, may improve engagement (Churkovich & Oughtred, 2002; Dewald, 1999; Nichols, Shaffer, & Shockey, 2003; Silver & Nickel, 2005; Viggiano & Ault, 2001; Yi, 2005; York & Vance, 2009).

Librarians attempt to engage learners on Blackboard (and other learning management systems) by adding different learning objects. A "learning object" is defined as "a piece of content that's smaller than a course" (Sosteric & Hesemeier, 2002). Some learning objects may include discussion board topics, diagrams, flowcharts, images, instructional videos, exercises, and quizzes. Some authors (Costello, Lenholt, & Stryker, 2004;

Jackson, 2007; Lenholt, Costello, & Stryker, 2003; Stone, Bongiorno, Hinegardner, & Williams, 2004; Xiao, 2010; York & Vance, 2009) recommend including library instructional content in Blackboard by incorporating modules such as instructions on how to locate sources, evaluate sources, cite sources, and distinguish between popular and scholarly sources. Some librarians include handouts to download and some embed the content into the actual Blackboard pages.

In Polger's experience, information literacy modules have also included practical learning objects in the Blackboard courses such as including instructions on how to access databases from home. Other examples are sample APA (American Psychological Association) citations as well as providing and explaining the components of an APA citation.

When developing online information literacy modules, instructional designers use the ADDIE model to develop effective learning objects (Davis, 2013; Webb & Hoover, 2015). Instructional design incorporates teaching theory, instructional practice, curriculum development, and assessment so that learners can learn effectively (Chapman & Cantrell, 2016). In the last 20 years, instructional design has embraced technology. More online courses are now developed and they incorporate instructional design principles. Instructional designers work alongside subject matter experts (SME) to develop online learning objects that best engage learners.

The ADDIE model is an instructional design framework that stands for analysis, design, development, implementation, and evaluation. This model is usually associated with the development of online learning objects such as interactive video tutorials, quizzes, charts, tables, graphs, diagrams, and Web pages. The ADDIE model is also used in the creation of those learning objects where stakeholders (i.e., students) are consulted before a learning object is created. The design is created and developed with the feedback from learners. This helps in keeping the learning object as engaging as possible. After implementation, more feedback is solicited so that the instructional designers can further improve the learning objects (Davis, 2013; Webb & Hoover, 2015).

Asynchronous versus Synchronous Online Learning

Online learning can occur in asynchronous and synchronous environments. To best engage learners, it is recommended to have synchronous learning activities such as live online chats, webinars, and live video conferencing (Branon & Essex, 2001; Hrastinski, 2008). There are advantages and disadvantages to both asynchronous and synchronous online learning and they have different effects on student engagement. It is important to note that while increased synchronous learning activities in online classes do increase learner engagement opportunities, they negate the flexibility of online learning. The authors recommend a balance of synchronous and asynchronous learning activities that balance the need for engagement and autonomous flexible online learning. When interviewing one librarian about her struggle because of her employer's insistence that she incorporate more synchronous learning into her online classes, she expressed her reservations because having a three-hour online lesson with the disembodied voice of an instructor can be very disengaging to any class, even though the class is online together at the same time. She commented that she did not know if learners who were logged in were actually engaged. She thought that a three-hour online synchronous class could be very limiting and restrictive to the learner. After an extended amount of time, the learner could get distracted and just start watching television or become involved in another activity.

The authors argue that asynchronous online learning is more convenient and flexible than synchronous online learning. Although synchronous online learning provides the maximum amount of engagement, it is very restricting and limiting to expect all learners to be online at the same time. It goes against one of the best qualities of online learning, which is that it is a more flexible type of learning. A compromise that some online instructors use in their teaching is to combine synchronous and asynchronous activities. An example of this may be live chats, which may be held once per week for one hour. Weekly live chats provide an opportunity for the class to get together and interact with each other. Video chats using Google Hangouts, Skype, Blackboard Collaborate, or GoToMeeting also provide some opportunities for live collaboration and interaction. However, using video chatting as a method to do synchronous online learning may post more obstacles such as time zone differences and technology problems. Some Web browsers might not support the video chatting software, while some online learners might be learning in time zones that might make coming together as a single class difficult. As an example, the online instructor might be teaching to the majority of their online learners in the eastern United States but she might be holding this class while vacationing in Europe so that while the class is happening during a convenient hour for the students she might be teaching in the middle of the night. The online learners do not need to know where she is exactly but the online instructor is very aware that it will be more challenging to hold a three-hour synchronous class when it is 3:00 a.m. for her (and 6:00 p.m. for her class).

Polger notes that when he was holding his online health libraries class live chat, he was dining at a local restaurant with friends while having a lively, engaged discussion with his class. He did feel guilty that he was using his mobile device in the restaurant, trying to balance his level of engagement with his online class and his conversation with his friends in the restaurant. Of course he was guilty of double booking his restaurant excursion with his friends with his live chat appointment with his learners. Synchronous learning opportunities are always something the online instructor strives for, but they are very restrictive and limiting to both the learner and the instructor.

Universal Design for Learning

Universal design for learning (UDL) is a concept that goes beyond simply the classroom. UDL is a pedagogical method used that encourages a diversity of teaching practices that focus on being inclusive to all types of learners. It does not represent a single way of teaching but includes various strategies that are more inclusive to a diversity of learning styles. According to the National Center on Universal Design for Learning (2014),

> Universal Design for Learning is a set of principles for curriculum development that give all individuals equal opportunities to learn. UDL provides a blueprint for creating instructional goals, methods, materials, and assessments that work for everyone—not a single, one-size-fits-all solution but rather flexible approaches that can be customized and adjusted for individual needs.

UDL focuses on three main components: the "what" of learning, the "how" of learning, and the "why" of learning. It also focuses on how instructors can be more inclusive in their instructional practices.

The first principle of UDL focuses on "what" the instructor is providing and the multiple ways the learner accesses the content. This might include providing notes on the board, providing chapter summaries, or consulting the textbook. The instructor may offer alternative ways of learning for either auditory or visual or kinesthetic learners. The instructor might provide options for how information is displayed. The instructor must additionally provide explanations and clarity on the vocabulary and the language of the materials. The "what" of learning also includes the formats of how the content will be taught to learners. Instructors are encouraged to use technology as a method to deliver the content to the students. The teacher should also provide background information on the topics learned and identify patterns and relationships between the topics and other concepts and the larger world. Providing multiple pathways and methods to access the content will result in having more engaged learners (Center for Applied Special Technology, 2011).

The second principle of UDL represents the "how" of learning. This second principle relates to the different assessment methods that provide evidence that a learner has learned the material. The "how" of learning can be illustrated when the instructor provides multiple methods of communication. If the instructor offers multiple options to access them, such as office hours, e-mail support, in-person communication, or texting, then learners will feel that their instructor is providing many different ways to help foster learning. Some instructors provide different methods for assessment such as in-class quizzes, group-based testing, computer-based tests, and take-home exams. This level of flexibility might help foster greater engagement in the course content since learners are provided with many options in order to succeed (Center for Applied Special Technology, 2011).

The third principle of UDL is the "why" of learning. This principle relates to how instructors engage learners in the classroom. It is important to note that all learners can be engaged differently. Some learners are highly engaged when the instructor places them in groups and asks learners to interact with each other. Other instructors engage their learners by having them work on their own and then asking them to write self-reflective journals. The third principle focuses on the instructor providing multiple options for engagement.

As academic librarians, we employ different engagement strategies that will work very well with some learners but others might not benefit from them. In Polger's required information literacy classes, he has used a competence-based information literacy lab assignment that must be completed using the learning management system (Moodle) in conjunction with searching databases. In his observations of this assignment (worth 20 percent of the final grade), learners were both engaged and motivated to complete it because they knew it was required to complete the course and they knew it was worth 20 percent of their final grade. Since this competency-based lab was not a "test" but more like an in-class activity, this fostered more group collaboration and engagement because learners worked together and helped each other out.

Darby (n.d.) examines nine principles of Universal Design for Instruction (UDI). These are:

1.   equitable use;
2.   flexibility;

3. simple and intuitive instructions;
4. perceptible information;
5. tolerance for error;
6. low physical effort;
7. size and space for approach;
8. a community of learners; and
9. instructional climate.

Equitable use (#1, above) relates to providing different ways learners can succeed. Darby (n.d.) gives the example of providing different question types in a midterm or final exam. Flexibility (#2, above) might often be characterized by not instituting hard deadlines but by providing more lenient due dates for assignments. Simple and intuitive directions (#3, above) relates to providing clear instructions that are easy to understand. Darby (n.d.) recommends providing grading rubrics and concept maps so that material is presented in a clear and concise format. Adding headings, subheadings, bulleted lists, and tables also makes the course material more simplified. For perceptible information (#4, above), Darby (n.d.) recommends that instructors provide learning materials through different outlets. It is recommended to provide both PowerPoint slides as well as typewritten notes on the course websites, as well as notes written on the Whiteboard. This strategy focuses on making information available for both visual and auditory learners. For tolerance for error (#5, above), Darby (n.d.) argues that instructors should provide course material that is both introductory and advanced. This can be done by providing introductory lessons plus outside readings to supplement the course material. Providing supplemental links on the course website also provides additional information for advanced learners. Low physical effort (#6, above) is how instructors reduce physical fatigue in the classroom. Providing coffee breaks during the lesson, mixing group work and individual exercises, and providing exercises that require a computer and some that require pen and paper may help to reduce physical fatigue. The expression "change it up" applies to #6 as it relates to providing different types of test questions so that learners can practice their critical thinking skills. Size and space for approach (#7, above) relates to changing the orientation of the classroom to facilitate better learning. Some classes work well when the desks are formed in a semicircular arrangement. A community of learners (#8, above) focuses on creating a community of learners who support each other and teach other. In this perspective, the instructor learns from the students as much as the students learn from their instructor. The instructor must create a supportive environment where all learners of all strengths support each other. The last principle of UDI is instructional climate (#9, above). Instructional climate relates to the overall setting of the class, from the temperature of the classroom to the seating arrangement of the desks. In Polger's information literacy classes held in the evening, he allows learners to bring food to class as he understands that many work full time and come straight to school afterward. He also allows students to take coffee breaks and he encourages learners to support each other (for extra credit). Fostering a supportive class environment makes the class more pleasant. In his freshman skills classes, Polger emphasizes the need for respectful disagreements between the students, especially when discussing sensitive topics such as racism in the United States. Polger constantly reminds learners that his classroom should be a place where all learners can express themselves and their behavior should not resemble a stereotypical New York City subway. Polger does not intend to be humorous but many of his learners find him funny. Providing a healthy class environment allows learners to feel comfortable enough so that they are their authentic selves.

Chodock and Dolinger (2009), Zhong (2012), and Webb and Hoover (2015) write about how UDL can be applied to information literacy classes. Chodock and Dolinger (2009) developed a new pedagogical method known as Universal Design for Information Literacy (UDIL). UDIL is culled from the nine principles of the UDI and it applies to the information literacy classroom. In their article, Chodock and Dolinger (2009) focus their study on learners with learning disabilities. They argue that librarians are already using UDI principles in their library instruction classrooms, but not consciously (Chodock & Dolinger, 2009, p. 30). Their main argument is that librarians should teach to the diversity of learners and not teach to one learner type. Web-based tools, as well as print and verbal communication, should be used to disseminate the material. Active learning should be used to engage learners. Chodock and Dolinger (2009) recommend the use of student-selected topics and the elimination of library jargon in their instruction. By presenting information in multiple formats and in small pieces, the information becomes less intimidating and overwhelming. Redesigning classroom space fosters collaboration and minimizes distractions (Chodock & Dolinger, 2009, p. 27).

Zhong (2012) applied UDL pedagogy to library instruction by describing how librarians can respond to the diversity of learning styles in their class by incorporating different ways to teach information literacy concepts. Zhong (2012) gives the example of Boolean searching, which is a difficult concept to teach. Usually librarians teach this concept verbally or graphically (e.g., by using Venn diagrams) but she argues that librarians can also teach it kinesthetically.

Zhong employs several methods for teaching Boolean searching such as providing the Venn diagram using PowerPoint slides that meet ADA standards, providing supporting websites, and providing verbal language. In addition, she provides a physical exercise that Polger also provides (Zhong, 2012). Providing different learning methods helps promote UDL.

In Polger's required information literacy classes, he teaches Boolean searching by asking all learners to stand up. Then he asks only the learners who are wearing baseball hats to remaining standing, and then he asks those who are wearing baseball hats and glasses to remain standing. This obviously works if there are learners who are wearing baseball hats and glasses or different colored clothing. The students easily understand when he uses a real-life example, as opposed to simply drawing circles on the board.

Library Tours for Incoming Students

Librarians can improve engagement during library tours by providing scavenger hunts tours, quizzes, prizes, popcorn, loot bags, and other incentives. Some tours are self-guided, other tours are virtually delivered on library websites, while other tours are given by external departments (e.g., the admissions department). Library tours that involve showing learners the facility may improve engagement as they are physically moving about the space and starting to understand the relationship between the physical building and the free services libraries offer that support college courses.

Library tours represent a great example for kinesthetic learning because learners are moving around and experiencing the library firsthand. By seeing the circulation desk and the reference desk, they can process the differences between each of these service desks. Since they are physically in the library, they have a better opportunity to learn. Instead of describing the reference collection, we can show them what a reference collection looks like.

During actual library tours, it is recommended to have a loose script (or guide) that will act as your lesson plan for the tour. Librarians must make the tours accessible to all, easy to understand, and fun. Some librarians use an informal tone when providing the tour while others are more formal and official. The authors recommend being informal and accessible. Incentives such as a certificate, USB flash drive, food, or swag (pens, stapler, highlighter) should be given so that learners have something to remember the tour and hence the library and the librarian. Having the tour visit multiple service points in addition to the circulation desk and the reference desk—for example, the library instruction classroom, the group study rooms, and the stacks—helps learners understand the different services the library provides to learners in college. In some instances, Polger has taken learners to the technology support center, a room where library staff lend out laptops and calculators. Throughout the tour, the central theme of learner support is mentioned and emphasized.

Providing connections to what learners already know, and building upon those connections, is a technique both authors employ in their library tours. For example, showing learners the color-coded call number map in Polger's library demonstrates that the library materials are arranged by call number and each call number range is assigned an aisle number, like in a department store or a supermarket. Teaching learners that call numbers represent a set of special codes (like a store's stock-keeping unit (SKU)) that organizes materials on a shelf helps them understand where to locate materials. More broadly, teaching learners that library materials are organized by subject, like how food is organized in a supermarket, helps them understand how materials are organized in a library.

During the tours, teaching the basics of call numbers may help incoming learners understand how libraries are organized and this may reduce library anxiety (Burhanna, Eschedor Voelker, & Gedeon, 2008; Sandy, Krishnamurthy, & Rau, 2009; Smith & Baker, 2011).

Librarians understand that learners use Google as their first tool to answer basic research questions. In his tours, Polger mentions that encyclopedias are the first places students should go when starting research. Even though students consult Google first, encyclopedias should be used to get a basic idea of a topic. Emphasizing that libraries provide credible and factual information to help students succeed makes it very clear as to why new incoming students are going on a library tour.

In Polger's experience, sometimes library tours are not possible due to staff shortages or other issues. In that case, Polger provides in-service presentations to several hundred learners at a time, which is not as engaging as presenting to a smaller group.

If Polger must present a PowerPoint to a mass of incoming learners, there are some techniques that facilitate learning and help keep learners engaged, even during potentially boring PowerPoint presentations (that both authors recommend avoiding).

Learning and Engaging—Using Boring PowerPoint Presentations

In Polger's experience, there are times when he must present a virtual tour using PowerPoint presentations. In those cases, he works with the New Student Programs Office on his campus and provides 45-minute presentations to 300 learners at a time in a theatre. Polger provides presentations in the morning and late afternoon. In his experience, he has learned to target a specific set of learning outcomes and avoid presenting too much information.

Obviously, when presenting a PowerPoint, it is recommended to avoid using too much text (as many learners do not want to read after a hearty lunch), so using realistic photos is more engaging. Polger has found that moving around and circling the auditorium works well to keep learners' eyes moving. Polger also starts the presentation with a series of questions.

Asking questions and creating an environment that encourages a dialogue (rather than a boring presentation) allow learners to have their voices be heard, and this helps them feel more involved in the discussion and more empowered. Making the presentation practical will motivate them to come to the library later. Summarizing the function of an academic librarian as helping learners succeed in college clearly identifies our role in college. It also teaches learners that librarians are involved in the college experience. In addition, it dispels the myth that we shelve books and sit at the reference desk all day looking up information on a database or library catalog.

During the PowerPoint presentation, Polger often focuses on the "services" of the library, rather than "showing off" the collection. Historically, the library's value was measured by the depth and breadth of its collection (Bonn, 1974; Evans, 1970; Orr, 1973). While students do not always understand it, the size of the library building is less important than the plethora of services offered in it. In the presentation, teaching learners that our services are free and they are tailored for their majors are critical talking points. Repeatedly emphasizing the high level of quality of information and the delivery of services represents an important part of the presentation. Connecting the familiar (i.e., Google) with the unfamiliar (our subscribed collection of databases) also helps them understand that both are similar.

In one of our interviews, one of the instruction librarians (Dr Naomi Gold) spoke about how we teach learners what databases are. In presentations to incoming learners, teaching them that they already are surrounded by databases like iTunes, Facebook, Twitter, Amazon, and

Instagram allows learners to understand the true nature of what a database is. As both authors are plain language advocates, they both try to avoid unnecessary jargon and use easy terms that learners will understand.

PowerPoint presentations can be more engaging if one embeds short videos (under 60 seconds) to supplement the discussion. Taking breaks to ask questions, in addition to connecting concepts to the real world, will add value to the presentation. The authors recommend the reader avoid reading the presentation and promote constant movement. This will reduce learner lethargy. Allowing the learners to have a voice and participate in the presentation will also improve learning and engagement.

Virtual Chat Reference

Polger often does more teaching during online chat reference sessions than at the physical reference desk where he is employed. Numerous articles discuss the best practices in the delivery of online chat (Ward, Mervar, Loving, & Kronen, 2013; Waugh, 2013). In order to best handle the online reference interview, some institutions collaborate with other colleges to provide online chat reference 24/7. Some colleges provide scripts to best handle the most popular questions and have training sessions on how to prepare canned messaging to speed up the process and ensure quality. Online chat reference is also improved by studies on conversation analysis and longitudinal research (Koshik & Okazawa, 2012; Kwon & Gregory, 2012; Radford & Connaway, 2013).

To best engage learners in an online environment, it is recommended to introduce yourself and acquaint the students with the structure of the library website at the start of the online chat. To be more acquainted with any possible reference questions, there is a knowledge base (i.e., database of learner inquiries) in the online chat reference software. A consistent dialogue should be implemented to best keep the flow of the reference interview. If there is a lag in the conversation, this could be due to a disconnection in the service, the learner has found his/her information and does not need us, or the learner is multitasking by searching on his or her own or texting or watching YouTube, and so on. It is not recommended to have a lull in conversation because that may decrease engagement. It is also not recommended to chat with multiple learners at the same time (although Polger is guilty of doing this). Finally, to keep the conversation going beyond online chat, the librarian might want to give his or her e-mail address as a follow-up, in case the online chat gets disconnected.

If your online chat reference service belongs to a consortium, it is best to become acquainted with the library websites of those colleges you are supporting (if those librarians are not providing chat reference). As an example, Polger participates in online chat reference that spans the entire United States. Polger uses QuestionPoint and some of the CUNY colleges also subscribe to QuestionPoint. This particular subscription is part of a larger network of college libraries that support each other 24/7. Polger prefers to answer questions in the evening when he gets home from work. He prefers the midnight timeslot for New York (9 p.m. in California). Polger enjoys answering chat reference questions from universities in California because he feels he receives more challenging questions and he enjoys navigating through different library websites. It is vital to learn the basic structure of other college library websites so that the learner experiences the same level of service as a librarian who is local.

Text Reference (SMS Reference)

Brooks and Zubarev (2012) discuss how John Jay College of Criminal Justice, a CUNY college, started its own text messaging (SMS) reference service by sharing a Blackberry device. Other articles also discuss the benefits of SMS reference service (Brannon, 2010; Cassidy, Colmenares, & Martinez, 2014; Cole & Krkoska, 2010; Gervasio, 2014; Kingsbury, 2015; Vecchione & Ruppel, 2012; Walsh, 2009). According to the Pew Research Center (Duggan & Rainie, 2012), 80 percent of cell phone owners use the SMS (texting) service to send or receive information. Text reference can be a great way to engage learners since communication is immediate and there is no lag, unlike e-mail. Texting is easy, offers patron privacy, and can be integrated into a Web-based interface or via a mobile device (Vardeman & Barba, 2014). Hill, Hill, & Sherman also found that patrons used text reference for simple questions since it requires the least effort. For more in-depth research questions, they found that most learners preferred in-person reference service rather than virtual reference services (Hill, Hill, & Sherman, 2007).

Text reference may be successful for teaching specific information literacy concepts in small bursts. Librarians must learn textspeak, which is abbreviated texting jargon most used by millennials (Cassidy et al., 2014). Texting reference might encounter some problems such as teaching more complex concepts that cannot be taught over one text. If librarians need to send multiple texts in order to teach a more complex topic, text reference might not the most engaging method for learners.

According to Pearce (2010), text reference service offered by NYU libraries offered no vendor-imposed limits since NYU libraries used their own Blackberry device to offer text reference. Text message conversation length depended on how engaged the learner was. Sometimes questions and responses were very brief and other times longer. The only logistical problem was carrying around a mobile device and not having a standardized and centralized location to assist learners. As NYU's text reference service developed, they integrated their text reference service with a Web-based instant message service, LibraryH3lp. Now librarians can answer text messages that get funneled through the same application as live chats using LibraryH3lp as the application (Pearce, 2010).

Both text reference and live chat reference may offer increased levels of engagement if librarians respond quickly, use abbreviated texting lingo, and teach concepts in small bursts. Providing too much information via texting or live chat can confuse and disengage the learner. Librarians must avoid using jargon and use simple and straightforward language. Similar to the reference interview, asking questions throughout the exchange also helps with identifying what the learner needs.

This chapter illustrates that since learning occurs beyond the library classroom, the librarian can seize this opportunity by successfully engaging the learners at their point of need. The next chapter explores the disappointment many instruction librarians face when they encounter a disengaged classroom. For many librarians, they feel like a failure. Some librarians blame an unsupportive and disengaged faculty member who sees library instruction as a field trip, while some librarians look to other external factors such as the time of the day, technology, the weather, or a small group of disruptive learners in class. There are so many variables that lead to disengagement. The following chapter examines a variety of the harmless, harmful, and sometimes toxic elements that may contribute to a perfect storm of disengagement.

CHAPTER SIX

Understanding Disengagement

Engagement does not always lead to learning. Seems like there may be confounding variables.

—Anonymous survey respondent

This chapter focuses on understanding disengagement and the multiple and confounding variables that might contribute to it. Classroom disengagement includes a wide spectrum of behaviors and might include ignoring the instructor and the subject matter by daydreaming, checking e-mail, texting, working on an assignment for another class, talking, or thinking about other things besides being present in the class. It is important to point out here that disengagement can work in two directions and either party in the classroom may be disengaged, faculty as well as the student. The library instruction session is just as greatly affected when the faculty member is disengaged as when the student is not engaged.

As librarians, we beat ourselves up when we feel we have not successfully engaged our students. We blame our teaching style, our level of enthusiasm, our technology, our classroom, the physical facility, the time of the day, the research topic, or even the Internet connection. It is important to realize that engagement happens when both the teacher and the learner are open to the classroom exchange. Student engagement occurs when there is a connection between the teacher, the content, and the learners involved.

Classroom Behavior

If students misbehave or if there are any disruptions in class, then engagement will be more difficult to achieve and maintain. A student texting in class might be quiet and not disruptive, but if the cell phone constantly beeps when new texts arrive, then that might have a negative impact on the overall atmosphere of the class. If the faculty member cannot control his/her class or does not enforce appropriate policies on classroom behavior, then the class cannot be engaged and the librarian will feel that their time is being wasted. An engaged class starts with an engaged faculty member who believes in the importance of visiting the library for a class.

Technology

Main (2004) addresses the trends for faculty to incorporate online components into their courses as a way to promote engagement. He cautions that incorporating too much technology may have a negative effect. He argues that although technology offers "the next best thing to being there" (p. 340), it might alienate the learner's experience. He argues that Web-based learning may have a negative effect on learning as it "facilitates physical isolation, surveillance, and inauthentic engagement" (p. 339). He also believes that incorporating technology in the classroom allows governments and educational institutions to have more control over students' behavior. Web-based learning often offers generic feedback on online quizzes and much of the content is not tailored to the individual learner. Main also argues that online learners may self-censor more because they fear their comments might be reported to the police or the FBI. He argues that incorporating technology may lead to a reductive system of binary logic (p. 342) and eliminate critical thinking. He argues that students who participate in secured Web-based learning (like Blackboard) may not be their authentic selves because they feel their comments might be made public. With learners having to log in multiple times to access their grades, their Web-based courses, their tuition bill, and their e-mail, institutional IT departments have created a barrier that actually fosters distrust and suspicion. This may actually affect learners' level of engagement in a negative manner. Similar to Facebook, some people may steer away from an engaged discussion because they fear their comments might be reported and their accounts closed.

Main argues that Web-based learning actually dumbs down learning by promoting a reductive effect, rather than encouraging critical and creative thinking. He argues that we should use Web-based instruction to supplement traditional classroom instruction, but not to replace it. He asserts his disappointment that in order to be professionally validated, faculty must include technology into their instruction, so they can be perceived as being "current." He also expresses concerns that students learn how to use technology so they can plagiarize without getting caught and that faculty must police their learners by putting their students' papers through plagiarism prevention software. Incorporating technology might help in providing different teaching methods, but it also might alienate learners in the process.

In Polger's information literacy classes (which are taught in person), he avoids using the Learning Management System (LMS) that are assigned to his classes (Moodle and Blackboard) because he believes it takes more class time to teach students how to use them. Teaching students how to use the LMS might alienate those who are not as tech savvy as others who are more comfortable with technology. Those who might be struggling to use the LMS might feel less engaged with the class overall than those who are more comfortable with technology.

In addition, Polger avoids using multiple-choice questions in his tests. Although easier to grade, multiple-choice questions cannot measure student learning. Multiple-choice questions actually serve as a way to increase disengagement. Many students randomly select the answers and they become disengaged with the course content and the test itself.

In the first week of Polger's required information literacy classes, all learners must complete a college-wide, multiple choice questionnaire. Polger administers this questionnaire (created by the college) and observes the problems with multiple choice questions. If many of his students do not understand the concepts, they randomly guess the responses. Many learners feel anxious that they do not understand the concepts addressed. Some begin to disconnect and randomly select answers without a deep critical analysis. This first week questionnaire is used as a way to assess their information literacy skills and learners are not graded. After the questionnaire, Polger goes through the questionnaire and discusses each of the questions and their responses and students provide feedback on how they interpret each response. He believes that multiple-choice questions do not provide enough insight on student learning and are used because they provide a superficial snapshot. Multiple choice questions are also easier to grade. In all of Polger's quizzes and tests, he only uses short answer questions. They provide an opportunity for learners to illustrate their level of understanding through their writing.

Sometimes there are external factors that affect the learning experience. The teacher might be unaware that there is an invisible obstacle that might affect learning. In the last few years, technology has greatly distracted the learning experience. Students who bring their laptops, tablets, and smartphones to class can easily hide their texting, Facebook, Twitter, Instagram, and shopping visits. With Google automatically installed on many people's smartphones, it is inevitable for them to surf the World Wide Web while in class. Technology is a distraction to learning because students feel the need to always be connected (Johnson, 2013). Many students do not want to miss out so they believe they can multitask by being in class, while texting, checking their e-mail, and using Facebook and other social media. Turkle (2015a) noticed that her students feel the need to be constantly connected. Even if some students are not using technology in class, if other students are using technology, then the instructor and the other students will be distracted. This may lead to a lack of engagement in the class. When students see others texting or shopping on Amazon, they feel that they could do the same. Turkle (2015a) writes that distraction is contagious. Technology, however, does not always lead to disengagement. Some students may use their smartphones to share their notes in class, thus increasing engagement while others are distracted (Reilly & Shen, 2011).

Polger has observed that when he holds information literacy classes in computer labs, he is often worried that students will be tempted by unfiltered Internet access. When he walks around the classroom to observe the students, he often notices multiple tabs opened. He notices that the students are working on their research papers and searching databases, while checking their e-mail and shopping on Amazon. He realizes that he cannot compete with the plethora of information on the World Wide Web. Sometimes, it is impossible to avoid disengagement. Multitasking is always perceived as a positive characteristic in professional work settings and in academic settings. However, experiments have shown that students who multitask on their laptops have scored lower on tests than students who have not multitasked (Fried, 2008; Ravizza, Hambrick, & Fenn, 2014; Sana, Weston, & Cepeda, 2013).

On one occasion, Polger's students were working on a lab assignment where they were required to search databases to find specific articles and then cite them in the American Psychological Association (APA) format. There was one keen student who wanted to complete the lab first and so worked hard to complete it on time, but then was bored having to wait for everyone else to finish up. Because every student works at different speeds, not all students will remain engaged together. Everyone cannot be engaged at all times.

A Warning about Trendy Engagement Techniques

Educators are always looking for new ways to teach so that students can learn better. Sheidlower believes that most of these trendy techniques, while they make sense theoretically and probably work in an ideal world or with groups of students who come from a richer, and therefore safer, socioeconomic backgrounds, they do not work very well with students from a lower, less stable socioeconomic class. Polger disagrees and does not believe class has anything to do with the techniques not working. His feeling is that these trendy ways of teaching require discipline on the part of the student. When they do not work, this is based upon the student's personality. Sheidlower agrees but thinks that when people are busy trying to eat and pay the rent, discipline of this kind is not "at the top of their list."

The three of these trendy techniques that will be written upon in this book are Google jockeying (see next section), when students choose the topic for their research paper and flipped classrooms (see Chapter 4).

Google Jockeying

Google jockeying can be both engaging and disengaging at the same time. To "google jockey" means that while the teacher is presenting, a student will google the specific topics that are being discussed in order to better understand the material (Educause Learning Initiative, 2006; Robb & Shellenbarger, 2012).

Google jockeying was invented in approximately 2006 by a professor at the Annenberg School for Communication at the University of Southern California who believed that students would be able to better follow along with his lecture if they googled the topics being discussed.

Google jockeying is initiated by having the instructor designate a student in class who plays the role of jockey. While the professor is teaching, the google jockey performs a series of Google searches that would accompany the lecture.

It might be used as a class activity to help increase learning, but it might hinder the student from actually learning the lesson, while he or she googles the material. It provides a multitasking test for the student, but in the end, the student may miss valuable content while he/she ventures off on his or her own into the Google universe. Some teachers might feel that they are competing with Google for the students' attention.

Too Much Lecturing?

There is a fine line between balancing what is taught and presented in class and what is left for "hands-on" experiential learning. If the librarian lectures for too long, students might fall asleep or lose attention. Library literature encourages incorporating discussion, interactive group work, activities, and, more recently, student response systems such as clickers and texting answers using SMS technology (Dill, 2008; Hoppenfeld, 2012; Osterman, 2008). The authors know that if they speak too much, some students start to fall asleep or their eyes gloss over. It is easier to manage disengagement with a 15-week semester class than with a one-shot library instruction session. In a one-shot session, the librarian does not really know the parameters of the students' attention span. Since the librarian is the "visitor" to the classroom, the student may not feel the need to be fully invested in being engaged. In most one-shot sessions, the librarian is not involved in the grading process. Since the act of grading places the faculty member in a position of power and authority, the student is more inclined to be more engaged in the faculty member's teaching versus the librarian's teaching, who is correctly perceived as an outlier. It is for this reason that it is important and useful that the class's actual professor remain with the class during the one-shot.

Students Choosing the Topic of the Research Paper

The idea behind students choosing a topic of a research paper by themselves is that, whatever topic they choose, they will be both extremely interested in and invested in and therefore they will do a better job of both writing and researching the paper. This Utopian idea sounds very good in theory, and while it can work, depending upon the topic chosen by the student, it also can be a fiasco. Students like doing this because, especially in college, they like to feel that they are in charge of their lives and education and they are being treated as adults. However, if undergraduates can choose anything, that means they can choose anything, even if it cannot be researched. For example, there is nothing to prevent them from choosing as their topic, "The effect of anime upon the original edition of the Gutenberg Bible."

In point of fact, students have approached both authors at their respective reference desks with unanswerable or unresearchable topics. While it is true that the topic of the paper is really under the purview of the student's classroom faculty, nonetheless it affects the student–librarian relationship. When the librarian explains to the student that the paper cannot be researched and the topic must be changed, the student may feel uncomfortable/upset/angry because suddenly the librarian is contradicting the classroom teacher. These feelings are verbalized as, "But my professor said. . . . " At the same time, the student can also feel alienated and disengaged.

This problem is easily managed. If a group of students approach the reference desk with undoable assignments, then the librarian can contact the professor to explain why they are undoable. Sometimes the librarian can then negotiate a doable assignment and sometimes the librarian will be taught by that professor how to do the assignment. An example of an undoable assignment being negotiated happened to Sheidlower when a class began approaching his reference desk wanting to look up articles in a specific database. Even though the librarian kept explaining that the college did not have access to that database, the students insisted they had to use it because that was the database the professor insisted that they use. Finally the librarian tracked that adjunct professor. The professor explained she really liked that database and used it all the time while working on her PhD. She said she was doing her degree at Princeton and that was where she used it. The librarian explained that the college they were both working for did not subscribe to that database and the students had no access to it. He suggested that the class use another database that the school had and it would get the results the professor wanted. Upon learning that the school had an alternate database available, the professor agreed to use it. The students were able to do their assignment from that point forward and hopefully they were more engaged in it because now it could be done. Wonderful example of why professors need to collaborate with the librarian before the research!

Online versus Face-to-Face Learning

Online learning, in the form of massive open online courses (MOOCs), Blackboard, Sakai, Desire2Learn, Moodle, or any one of the myriad other asynchronous learning management systems that exist, might not foster engagement as well as "face-to-face" learning. When using these systems, students are isolated and must create the excitement of learning by themselves. They also are boxed into one type of learning, since the lesson has been previously created by the faculty member. In a "face-to-face" classroom, the faculty member can use his or her instantaneous understanding of what is going on in the room to tweak the material's presentation. For example, if students look bored or are not paying attention, the instructor might choose to insert a joke or a topical reference (such as something from campus life, as in "you know our baseball team tonight will win because they are aware of this particular physics formula") to catch the students' attention. Unfortunately, this cannot be done with a "pre-packaged asynchronous learning management system."

Polger teaches an online medical libraries course at Mohawk College in Hamilton, Ontario, Canada. Each week he encourages his students to participate in discussions using the weekly discussion board topics. Unfortunately, due to the asynchronous nature of the online course, it has been difficult to engage the class. It is only twice per month when the students meet in real time to have their live online chat, when the class actively participates in discussion. Over the years, Polger has noticed that live online chats have always been a forum where the most active, engaged discussions have taken place. Most of the learners in the class (about 15 students) understand that these online live chats are required for their 5 percent participation grade. But it is difficult to get all learners together (online) at the same time as the very nature of online learning is about promoting flexibility.

Polger's friend, Dr. Naomi Gold, teaches an online synchronous class. She worries that her class may suffer fatigue and disengagement because her class is synchronous and held for three hours at a single time. What appears to be the perfect opportunity for the ultimate experience in online engagement might be exhausting for students to remain engaged (online) for three hours at a time.

Attitude of Classroom Faculty in the Library Classroom

The attitude of the classroom faculty who brings the class to the library sets the tone for how engaged students will be. Since the classroom professor gives the grades, undergraduates often take their lead from this faculty member. If the faculty member is late, cannot manage his/her class, is texting during the entire library instruction session, or not paying attention in some other very obvious manner, then this shows a lack of engagement (and respect) toward the librarian's presentation and teaching. In the authors' experiences, students tend to treat the librarian in whatever manner their professor treats the librarian. If the session is a joke and unimportant to the faculty member, then it will be a joke and unimportant to the students as well. But if the faculty member is engaged as well as the students and paying attention, so too will members of the class be engaged and pay closer attention.

If students observe the classroom faculty continuously interrupting the librarian, dismissing the librarian's lesson, and not taking the library instruction seriously, this attitude may extend to students. Student engagement does depend on the teacher's behavior, and vice versa (Kotter, 1999; Skinner & Belmont, 1993). Faculty members must advocate the importance of library instruction to their students, to their colleagues, and to their department heads. Since the library department within the college setting is considered a service department, some faculty do not perceive librarians as professionals (and in some cases, faculty). This sometimes leads to a level of faculty elitism. The librarian might be perceived as a threat to the faculty member and the faculty member can be very territorial when it comes to his or her class and class time. This might materialize in a subtle power struggle between the librarian and the faculty member. In most cases, the librarian's role is perceived of as subservient to the faculty member.

In one recent instance, Polger provided library instruction to a first year college composition class, and the teaching faculty member provided an assignment that was very challenging for first year students. Polger believed the assignment was inappropriate for a first year student but did not share his concerns with the faculty member. Like many other librarians, he thought it was not in his place to critique the research assignment presented to him. This assignment involved searching exclusively for peer-reviewed journal articles. The class in question had no experience recognizing, reading, or evaluating peer-reviewed journal articles. Many first year students struggle with understanding peer-reviewed journal articles, thus providing a challenge for the librarian. Many students self-identify as expert searchers, but if they do not understand what they are reading, then their level of engagement will be greatly affected. Despite this disconnection, librarians should provide instruction with the complete awareness that students might be ill-prepared for the class.

Content of the Class

While some librarians are teaching a full 15-week course at their institutions, a large percentage still teach one-shots at their institutions. Obviously when it is a 15-week course, then the content of the lesson is dictated by the syllabus and the curriculum. A one-shot is tailored to the subject of the class being taught. Both Polger and Sheidlower agree that the more closely the lesson is crafted to the assignment that the students are working upon, the more closely they will pay attention and hence the more fully they will be engaged. If there is no assignment, then the level of engagement falls greatly. When Sheidlower was the head of information literacy at York College, one of the rules was that if there was no assignment related to that class, then it would not be taught even if there was a librarian to teach it. This is very commonly practiced by high school librarians. Sheidlower felt that the quality of the assignment was not something that the librarian judged because if the librarian decided what the quality of the assignment was, then that would mean that the librarian was passing judgment upon the professor teaching the class, but there had to be an assignment. The only exception to this was if the faculty gave an assignment based upon resources that the students could not necessarily access. Then Sheidlower believes that it is the librarian's job to advocate for the student. A single doable assignment gives the students, the subject professor, and the librarian a common language, a common platform from which to speak, and a common meeting ground that all can participate in.

Librarians as Babysitters

A class will automatically be less engaged if the faculty member treats the librarian as a babysitter and the library instruction session as a field trip. The class will tend to be more engaged if the faculty member is engaged and takes the librarian and library lesson seriously. Since the librarian is the "guest," he or she is not respected in the same way as the instructor who holds the authority in grading the students. The investment in the library instruction session and the librarian "guest" are not as valued because librarians are not grading students. Student engagement would likely increase if librarians were respected by a faculty members who are library advocates.

The literature on librarians as babysitters mostly addresses public libraries and not academic libraries (Smith & Rivera, 2004). If the classroom faculty member is like the "parent" for the students, very often he or she might want to take the students to the library as a "field trip" and, in few cases, drop the students off in the library classroom for their library instruction class. This is a prime example of how disengagement can occur. If the classroom faculty does not stay with his/her class, it can be perceived as not only disrespectful but it might give a signal to his/her class that the library instruction session is not of high importance. Many librarians, including the authors, will cancel a library instruction class if the classroom faculty member leaves the classroom. It sends a message that librarians are not babysitters.

Tension between Library Instructor and Faculty Member

There is a subtle tension between the library instructor and the faculty member that should be discussed and acknowledged. The library instructor is the "guest lecturer" and some faculty might feel territorial about a librarian visiting their class and taking valuable time away from their semester. Faculty might also not approve of the librarian's teaching style or library lesson. Librarians see faculty as the subject matter expert and we see ourselves as the research experts (Biggs, 1981; Julien & Given, 2003; Kotter, 1999).

Faculty members often want the librarian to teach the class their way and the librarian is more knowledgeable as to the appropriate databases and appropriate research topics for lower level classes. Polger recounts how he wanted to promote the database "Opposing Viewpoints in Context" as an easy searching tool for a basic 100-level college writing class (as opposed to the database JSTOR, which he thinks is not as user friendly) and the faculty member did not allow her students to use the easier database. There needs to be a fair negotiation between librarian and faculty member that results in a shared understanding of each other's expertise. Faculty sometimes dismiss librarians and treat them as second-class professionals in the institution. At both the authors' institutions, the City University of New York (CUNY) where librarians are faculty, even classroom faculty are often unaware that librarians are their peers. Some treat librarians as assistants in their class, rather than as equal partners. Some faculty are very defensive of their turf (their classes and students) and some are not receptive to the expertise of the library instructor. Very often the librarian who is teaching the instruction session will need to seek approval on the research topics that are demonstrated or the overall flow of the class. It is not an equal partnership between colleagues, but a slightly tense working relationship where the librarian needs to engage both the student and the faculty member in a one-shot session.

Unlike a 15-week semester course, the librarian does not have a second chance to make a lasting impression. Some faculty members are uneasy "sharing" their class with a librarian. They have unrealistic expectations that a librarian can cover a semester's worth of concepts and appropriate "hands-on" learning in 90 minutes. Librarians must obtain enough buy-in from the faculty member to be embedded (online or in-person) to request a follow-up class to a one-shot. Engagement is very limited and challenging in a one-shot library instruction scenario.

Embedded librarianship might provide a solution for the problematic "one-shot" library instruction session but librarians are still often seen as the "guest," rather than as a teaching partner. Whether they are embedded on a learning management system such as Blackboard, or embedded in person through a series of several library instruction sessions, the librarian is not fully a member of the class. In an Association of College and Research Libraries conference presentation, Morrison and Garcia (2011) discuss that engagement can be further increased if the librarian is fully integrated in the classroom. Including librarians' names on the syllabus and having them listed as co-teaching the class, or listed on the course roster, might increase students' level of engagement.

Librarian Involved in Grading

Engagement will likely increase when the librarian is teaching to a specific research assignment. If students know there will be a specific outcome for the library class, they will listen more actively and pay more attention (Daugherty & Carter, 1997). If students were made aware that the library instruction session involved a library assignment where the librarian would be involved in grading, and would be assisting in grading the assignments themselves, then students would take the lesson more seriously. Their desire to succeed in class is often represented in their grades. To students, grading is the currency of success and faculty use it to objectively quantify students' capabilities. Students use their grades to classify themselves and sometimes one's grades represent part of the components of how a person formulates his or her identity as a college student.

A Class without an Assignment

If students come to the library instruction classroom without an assignment, it is more difficult to engage them. Polger argues that providing a library instruction class without an assignment is more promotional, rather than pedagogical. A class without an assignment decreases the student's motivation to connect with the class (Seamans, 2002). Some librarians create an artificial assignment to help motivate students in their classes (Galvin, 2006). Some librarians dread presenting a class without an assignment as some feel it will lead to a class of silent, disinterested students. For the librarian, a library instruction class that lacks an assignment should not be considered a lost cause. It may provide an excellent opportunity to promote the library to that specific target audience, while discussing the larger concepts of credibility, authority, and bias when conducting academic research.

Using Faculty Class Time

Teaching faculty are very protective of their class time. Some are reluctant to "give up" a full class hour to the librarian who will be presenting at that time. This attitude of reluctance can be subtle and sometimes it even can be not so very subtle as it is relayed to the students. This tension between the librarian and the classroom professor is sometimes conveyed to the class and might create a barrier between the librarian and the class. The end result of this barrier is a lack of engagement on the part of the class. This may result in an uphill battle that is not unusual in librarian–faculty interactions. Librarians and classroom faculty attempt to negotiate their teaching practices and the limited time constraints both have with their learners. Class time is a commodity and the librarians feel that they do not have enough time to teach and very often classroom faculty are unwilling to give up more time to the librarians. Partnering may be the answer.

As already observed, most librarians provide library instruction sessions in the form of one-shot workshops; students see the librarian for a limited amount of time, from 50 minutes (at Sheidlower's institution) to 2 hours (at Polger's institution). It will always be challenging to engage students in such a short period of time (Bean & Thomas, 2010). There is more literature that focuses on increasing the one-shot model as a means of improving student learning and engagement (Gandhi, 2005; Kvenild & Calkins, 2011).

Adjunct Faculty versus Full-Time Faculty

Full-time faculty are generally perceived as being more invested, engaged, and committed to their academic institutions. Adjunct faculty are not on the tenure track, not permanent, not on as many committees, and not as active in campus activities as full-time faculty. Some adjuncts tend to be "in transition," that is, on the lookout for a full-time opportunity. They may be teaching at many institutions and their loyalties might be unclear (Hoyt, 2012; Wyles, 1998).

In addition, because of their poorer pay, adjunct faculty may not be fully supported by their department and they may not be as fully engaged with their students as full-time faculty are (Fagan-Wilen, Springer, Ambrosino, & White, 2006). Some may feel a sense of resentment and may feel invisible when it comes to the politics of the institution. Depending upon the campus, when it comes to library instruction, adjunct faculty may be expected to teach the bulk of the undergraduate courses (overall) in the college. It must be acknowledged that at both authors' CUNY campuses, more adjunct faculty bring their classes for library instruction. Librarians often wish to target full-time faculty when promoting information literacy to the academic departments with which they liaise. However, it is worthwhile to target adjunct faculty as well. Full-time faculty might be overwhelmed with their research and some might be given a lighter teaching load. Since full-time faculty might not be teaching as many courses as adjuncts, they might be less engaged in the information literacy needs of their students.

Polger targets adjunct faculty because they represent the majority of all library instruction classes during the academic year. The reality is that many full-time faculty would rather teach more challenging, upper-level classes. In the case of both authors' employer (CUNY), many full-time classroom faculty are cross-appointed to teach graduate level courses at CUNY's graduate school as well as the undergraduate campuses.

External Factors

From the experience of a community college librarian, time of day (afternoon classes) has the greatest effect on student engagement. If it's late afternoon and the classroom is warm, it's much harder to engage students. I've also noticed that students are more indifferent when they know their professor sees no value in this session (e.g., the professor's chair is insisting on the students having a: "library orientation"). ("Instruction Librarians and Student Engagement Questionnaire," January 12, 2015)

Anyone who has ever taught early on a Saturday morning or even early in the evening after 5 p.m. or during lunch time has probably noticed that students are less attentive. The librarian must keep in mind that this has little or nothing to do with either the teaching style or with the content of the lesson. It has to do with the librarian being a stranger and with the time not being propitious. The time of year could also affect students' attention spans. Some students will suffer from seasonal affective disorder, a type of depression that affects about 6 percent of the adults in the United States alone (Targum & Rosenthal, 2008). Basically, it occurs during the autumn and the winter months and as such it would cover the fall semester. As a form of depression, it would definitely sap away students' attention during those months. There is little that can be done except, since it is related to the reduction in light during those months, to teach in as bright a classroom as is possible.

Time is not the only reason students are disengaged. If a student is hungry, tired from a long day of work, needs to use the restroom, depressed, anxious, angry, or distracted, that will greatly affect his or her level of engagement as well.

Macheski, Buhrmann, Lowney, and Bush (2008) attempt to reduce disengagement in their sociology classes by creating a community of learners. They accomplished this by creating a partnership between students, the faculty member, and the subject. This community is built on classroom interactions both in and out of the classroom (Macheski et al., 2008, p. 44). With the diversity of student personalities, some students learn best independently and prefer to work on their own, rather than in groups. Some students do not feel confident to work on their own, so they prefer to work in teams. As an example, if one student has difficulty expressing him- or herself in English, he or she might partner up with a native English speaker.

In a course with an online component (i.e., Blackboard) and where information literacy is incorporated into the course, Polger asks students to post to the online discussion boards as a way of increasing participation. Online discussions may help improve student engagement as some students might be too shy to participate in class, so they prefer posting online.

Washor and Mojkowski (2014) discuss 10 factors that affect engagement in young people. Students are often disengaged due to:

1. their perception of how committed their teachers are in their learning,
2. their inability to connect concepts learned in class with their future careers,
3. their inability to choose their courses,
4. their inability to feel challenged,
5. their inability to recognize the value of their school work,
6. their inability to apply what they have learned to the real world,
7. their fear of failing,
8. their inability to practice what they have learned in class,
9. their anxiety of not having enough time to learn and their own pace, and
10. their inability to learn at their own pace.

The authors conclude that schools are not flexible enough in asking teachers to teach to different students' learning styles and connecting course concepts to real-world problems and their future careers.

Black (2003) focuses on the external factors that affect student disengagement. She cites unsupportive neighborhoods, socioeconomic status, and malnutrition. She also found that student disengagement increases with age. Younger children are more enthusiastic and energized to learn but that decreases as students get older. She argues that some teachers use token rewards such as pizza parties or coffee and doughnuts. Polger brings munchkins and coffee for his students' final exam for his information literacy classes to create a positive environment and to dissuade his students from cheating.

Using external rewards such as pizza parties may have a positive effect on student learning, but according to Mader (2009), students need to be internally motivated first and foremost. Giving rewards to students to encourage learning might actually hinder learning because it may be perceived as "bribery" and may be perceived as manipulative (Mader, 2009; Levine & Fasnacht, 1974). The practice of good teaching and the use of verbal rewards may increase student engagement, rather than giving tangible rewards (Mader, 2009).

Millennials (Gen Y)

Millennial learners are more independent, self-confident, and autonomous, and they multitask (see also Chapter 2 for more about millennials). They always wish to be wired to their electronic devices and they might have difficulty with keeping attention on one thing at a time. They might feel distracted faster, and engagement could be more challenging with this group of learners. Unlike earlier generations, "learning for knowledge's sake" does not particularly interest or engage them.

Lang (2014) argues that teachers should not be blaming students for being disengaged, but they should consider incorporating games into their teaching in order to prevent disengagement. Incorporating games (Grassian & Trueman, 2007) such as the virtual reality game, Second Life might engage students but some students might not be excited about the concept of playing games in college. The elements of competition and role-play might engage some learners who enjoy gaming but not all learners.

Attitude toward Learning

One of the survey participants noted that disruptive students hinder their "ability to remain enthusiastic" and the classes' engagement can be affected by one person's attitude "which in turn affects the quality of my instruction" (anonymous questionnaire respondent, October 5, 2015). If a student is disruptive, then Sheidlower always asks him or her if that person wishes to teach the class. If the student says yes, then Sheidlower sits down and lets them. Basically, this is all a librarian can do. The faculty member is in the class to help control discipline of the class. If he or she will not do this, then the librarian must give up. All the librarian can do is to tell whoever scheduled the class that this class will not be or should not be rescheduled. Whenever a cell phone would go off in his class, Sheidlower would immediately stop teaching and start dancing to the ringtone. When the student started speaking on the phone, he would join in the conversation and encourage the class to join in as well. The class would understand what was going on and discipline the student. Cell phone only went off once in Sheidlower's class.

On the other hand, Polger sets the stage at the beginning of his 7.5 week and 15-week information literacy classes that he teaches at CUNY and ASA College. If any of his students need to use their cell phone for texting or speaking, they are encouraged to take their own coffee break and leave the classroom to attend to their phone calls. He also asks all students to turn their phones off or switch to vibrate. If a phone goes off during a class, Polger stops the class.

There are many reasons why a student might be disengaged and we often blame ourselves for not teaching "well enough." However, there are so many external factors that affect engagement. The entire class could be disengaged if they have an instructor who cannot control his or her own class. When they visit the library for an information literacy session, students might be completely disengaged because they have been this way throughout the entire semester and this one-shot library instruction just represents another class for them. The librarian and classroom faculty member must be active partners in engaging their learners. Librarians should not beat themselves up if some learners (or the entire class) are disengaged. An engaged classroom is like baking a cake. It comprises a recipe of many different ingredients that must be mixed together in the right order at the right temperature and using the correct proportions. Even the best baker can make errors when baking a cake. Even the most enthusiastic instructor can have difficulty engaging the learners, and as Sheidlower points out, sometimes it is more appropriate to end the class early or just stop the presentation and allow the class to work on their research assignment.

In the final chapter, the authors illustrate engagement as a set of behaviors and practices used to promote information literacy to classroom faculty. The chapter focuses on how librarians can incorporate engagement as part of their marketing strategy when promoting information literacy as a fundamental part of a learner's college education.

CHAPTER SEVEN

Marketing Information Literacy through Successful Engagement Practices

Librarians' collaboration with faculty may be one of the most important strategies that improves student engagement in an information literacy class.
—Anonymous survey respondent

The authors believe that incorporating engagement as a strategy is effective when marketing an information literacy program. At Polger's institution where he is employed full-time, he and several colleagues developed a library marketing campaign that promotes the library's credit course, one-shot library instruction sessions, and first year library workshops. Engagement as a practice can easily be integrated into the library's marketing plan.

Engagement and marketing go hand in hand. Without successful marketing, library users are not likely to be engaged. If academic libraries represent the heart of the campus, it should be a priority for librarians to engage their users so that they feel it is like another home for them. Since the library is at the same time both a "place" and a "service/resource," engagement should be included in the library's marketing plan (Montgomery & Miller, 2011). If users are not engaged, then, additionally, potential advocates who understand the value of the library will be lost. This chapter addresses how engagement should be a planned function in teaching and how it should be included as part of the library's marketing strategy.

Marketing the library represents a fundamental part of our jobs as librarians. In the library classroom, librarians are not only teaching but also promoting services, resources, and themselves. Explained in this way then, marketing should be seen as part of a larger process in connecting users with services and resources. The American Marketing Association defines "marketing" as the "the activity, set of institutions, and processes for creating, communicating, delivering, and exchanging offerings that have value for customers, clients, partners, and society at large" (American Marketing Association, 2013).

Marketing is used to connect users to products and services. It involves a long-term strategic plan that involves market research, targeting a specific audience (i.e., segmenting), promotion, communicating your message, and conducting more market research. Developing a successful connection and relationship with your audience can take many years. The marketing process is cyclical and it involves long-term planning and buy-in. Marketing also can be used in the classroom as an approach to engage students.

Often, librarians are unaware that they are involved in the marketing process. In the classroom, when highlighting a library's service or a resource, or mentioning extended hours, a component to the marketing process is being added. Done well, marketing must be subtle, selective, and targeted, and must not come across with the heavy hand of a used car salesperson. Librarians need to be mindful and to carefully curate what they promote. For example, asking undergraduate students how they watch movies helps properly promote the video collection. In this instance, students could share how much they love Netflix or YouTube. This valuable data would help to identify a service, such as a streaming video collection, like the Films on Demand commercial database, to promote to students. Many students love using Wikipedia when starting their research. Explaining to them that the Gale Virtual Reference Library database is just like Wikipedia may make them feel less anxious about using it when conducting research. Following are some promotional techniques that one can use in the classroom to help engage students.

Engaging Faculty before the Class

As Polger and Okamoto (2012) discuss, consulting faculty members before a library instruction session engages them in the process of creating a tailored, assignment specific session that is targeted to both their students' learning and research needs. By asking questions and soliciting feedback, the faculty member becomes more involved in the development of the library instruction class. When students come to class knowing that the library instruction session is not generic but targeted to their assignment or research topic, they feel more motivated and hence engaged. It also shows the students that the librarian is making an effort and is not creating a generic lesson plan but has created a subject specific tailored session with a customized handout that is targeted to a specific course level (100, 200, 300), a specific user group (psychology students who meet at 1:00 p.m. with Professor Smith), and a specific assignment (a cognitive psychology annotated bibliography).

At both of the authors' institutions, Polger and Sheidlower each provide library instruction to general education first year college composition classes. Enquiring before the class and asking if the students are English language learners (ELLs) (i.e., ESL students) helps greatly so that the librarian can tailor the class and communicate effectively. Neither author possesses a master of TESOL degree but being informed before the class that their learners are ELLs allows them to prepare to engage the faculty member and the students before the class is even held.

Engaging Students by Using Food to Promote the Facility

In a classroom, librarians have a great opportunity to promote the facility, not only as a learning environment, but as a social meeting space (Webb, Schaller, & Hunley, 2008). On some college campuses, the library is located in the center of campus. It should be promoted as the heart and brain of the institution and have an inviting entrance and flexible policies that engage students further. Promoting final exam weeks with extended hours helps raise the profile of the library but it might be more engaging if the library had therapy dogs, free coffee, and were more flexible about bringing food into the library (Bell, 2013; Foster, 2008). In Polger's 15-week information literacy classes, he provides coffee and donuts during the final exams. During the semester, he allows students to bring meals to class, as long as they clean up after themselves. This experience of being flexible makes students feel more welcome. It is an uphill battle to prohibit food in the library, especially when more libraries are allowing food in designated areas, as well as at their programming and events (Karle, 2008; Knapp, 2004; Mitchell, 2008).

Upon an analysis of the Association of College and Research Libraries Library Marketing and Outreach Facebook group (https://www.facebook.com/groups/acrl.lmao/), Polger found that many libraries engage with their users through various programs (that includes food) as part of their library marketing plan. Many libraries provide coffee and candies during final exams, despite the fact that many libraries have a "no food" policy. Much of the marketing strategies and events that libraries develop include refreshments as a way to draw users in.

Since the facility represents a meeting space, a social space, a study space, and a community space, it makes sense to embrace food as an engagement strategy in order to best promote the library as a welcoming space.

Engaging Students by Promoting Databases

In our classes, we are not only teaching but we are also promoting our value. Library promotion can be thought of as something that involves raising awareness on something specific that will benefit your audience. Graduate students who are writing a thesis or dissertation will greatly appreciate the librarian promoting RefWorks or Endnote. Upper-level undergraduate students in the humanities would appreciate the consultation services promoted in classes differently than upper-level science students. First year college students might not even know that there is a librarian on campus to help them.

While librarians are teaching, they should be mindful about what they promote. Whether the presentation is scripted or improvised, learners will not be engaged if assumptions are made about them. For example, it is important to ask the students how they get their news before one promotes the *New York Times* database.

Since learning is a two-way street, the way to couple marketing and learning with engagement is by asking questions and learning from your audience. Since many students prefer using Google, librarians may consider using the word "search engines" instead of "databases." For psychology majors, emphasizing that databases cost thousands of dollars may not be as effective as promoting PsycINFO as the "best search engine" for psychology students. It's important to emphasize that it's not a freely available website but a "private website" that the colleges pays to support college students' success. Specific databases can be promoted as "your best friend for research," or by saying "it's just like Google but of better quality." Promoting Gale Virtual Reference Library (GVRL) as an "academic version of Wikipedia" allows students to understand the differences between Wikipedia and GVRL.

Making comparisons to Google or Wikipedia are ways to promote library databases because students are already engaged with those websites. There is no need to promote Google or Wikipedia because students already make use of these, even though students are prohibited to use them for research by most instructors. Engagement is likely to increase when marketing is more selective and catered to their immediate, specific needs. Promoting a library database record by making comparisons with Facebook profiles might help students understand the nature of a bibliographic citation. Many students are already engaged with using Facebook, so connecting what they already know (a Facebook profile) with a database record might help them understand the nature of the components of a citation on a database. In class, showing them both Facebook profiles and database citations side by side might improve their level of engagement with using commercial databases as opposed to using Google (Polger & Okamoto, 2014).

Marketing Services in Class

Many students benefit from the array of library services offered from their college library. If your college's mission is to promote interlibrary loan by targeting graduate students and faculty, then it is best to promote interlibrary loan in graduate-level library instruction classes. If your library's assessment data show that most consultations are provided to upper-level undergraduate students, then your consultation service is best promoted to upper-level classes, as opposed to first year classes. Marketing services should be planned, have tangible goals, be targeted, thoughtful, organized, and logical.

Marketing Ourselves

Many students are unaware that liaison/subject librarians exist to support academic departments. Promoting college librarians as academic subject specialists to their majors will have a positive impact in the classroom. Students might become more interested in the session if they knew that there was a librarian who specialized in their major (Jaguszewski & Williams, 2013; Rodwell & Fairbairn, 2008).

Librarians can also make the class more engaging by developing their own brand of teaching. Colorful handouts, dressing up in costume, enthusiasm that might be dramatic or theatrical can increase student engagement in the classroom.

In librarians' consultations, Polger gives out his business cards. He hopes that they do not get thrown out. Business cards represent a small part of the marketing process, and it is always the hope that the students keep the librarians' cards handy in case they need to contact them. During consultations, sending materials to students from our work e-mails also promotes ourselves through our e-mail signature. The e-mail signature represents a more subtle way of letting the student know that we are only a "reply" away.

Developing a dramaturgical approach to teaching library instruction also helps in the engagement process. As Macfarlane (2007) discusses, teaching is a performance and the classroom represents the theater and students are your audience and the metaphoric space where teaching takes place is your stage. Goffman's (1959) dramaturgical approach of front-stage versus backstage behavior extends to teaching because librarians are mostly exhibiting front-stage behavior. Similar to publicists who communicate a favorable public image of a celebrity, front-stage teaching performance must incorporate library promotion, pedagogy, and engagement. Teaching can be tiring, especially when trying to impart all three.

Develop an Engaging Marketing Plan

In developing a strategic marketing plan, it might be a good idea to get users involved throughout the process. Brock and Tabaei (2011) discuss how their library collaborated with their marketing class on campus in order to develop the beginnings of the library's marketing plan. Wallace (2004) discusses engagement as a central part of the library's marketing plan.

Marketing and engagement go hand in hand because marketing cannot be successful unless users are engaged. An engaging marketing plan might include examples on how the library may partner with other campus departments, such as academic advisement (Benefiel, Arant, & Gass, 1999; Deuink & Seiler, 2006; Deuink & Seiler, 2009). Students who might be good candidates as library advocates might be student employees, students who are majoring in marketing, members of student government, and student employees who are part of the new student orientation team. This would be a group of highly engaged and involved students who are more active in implementing change, are more outspoken, are more comfortable with public speaking, and might be future activists. As discussed in detail later, an engaging marketing plan focuses on tailoring to its users and soliciting feedback and using market research data in order to successfully promote services and resources. Without consulting data, marketing can be neither successful nor engaging.

Advisory Committees

Developing an advisory committee of students, faculty, and librarians may help in the process of obtaining valuable data about users (Benefiel,

Arant, & Gass, 1999; Deuink & Seiler, 2006, 2009; Kaser, 1982; Smith & Galbraith, 2011). Polger recounts the development of a library advisory committee when he was a medical librarian in Toronto, Canada. The advisory committee consisted of stakeholders who use the library and who represent potential advocates. Since marketing relates with connecting people, products, promotion, price, and placement, it is critical for librarians to assess the needs of users (people). Without communicating with their audience and the various subgroups, librarians cannot successfully engage users. Successful marketing should lead to a more engaged audience.

Focus Groups

There is a body of library literature that argues that libraries cannot be successful without the use of focus groups (Sen, 2006; Höglund, 2014; Tobias & Blair, 2015; Yi, Lodge, & McCausland, 2013). Focus groups represent a specific method in marketing research. A targeted group of people get together to discuss a particular issue, and they propose various solutions. Focus groups are used to cull and interpret qualitative or quantitative data. Focus groups can be used to assess all library services. There is much literature on best practices in revamping library signage (Berger & Hines, 1994; Bosman & Rusinek, 1997; Polger & Stempler, 2014), redesigning library websites (Battleson, Booth, & Weintrop, 2001; Seeholzer & Salem, 2011), renovating library space, and providing other library services.

Focus groups represent powerful data for libraries. They represent a more user-centric way of running a successful library. Many librarians think they know best how to serve the user but multiple studies find a disconnect between what librarians think their users want and what library users actually expect or want in their libraries (Clark & Wallin, 1999; Crowley, Leffel, Ramirez, Hart, & Armstrong, 2002; Hiller, 2001; Massey-Burzio, 1998; McGillis & Toms, 2001; Montanelli & Stenstrom, 1999; Ouellette, 2011; Polger, 2011; Wilson, 1995; Young & Von Seggern, 2001). In addition to structured focus groups, questionnaires, informal conversations, and anecdotal evidence can provide valuable data that can be used to create changes that will improve services and create a more user-centered environment.

New Student Orientations: Engaging New Students as Part of Marketing

If the library is involved in new student orientation (Rhoades & Hartsell, 2008), library tours can be made more engaging using the following methods.

1. During the library tours, stop and ask questions. Ensure that everyone is paying attention, and ensure that there is a no texting/cell phone use during library tours.

2. Be selective and do not give too much information on tours. Information overload leads to a lack of engagement.

3. As part of the marketing plan, award students with promotional items that are branded with the library logo. This will help them remember the library and keep a useful piece of swag like a pen, stapler, mouse pad, and stickers, around.

4. If the library has a marketing budget, hand out library swag such as branded staplers, pens, stationery, branded mouse pads, USB flash drive, key chains, and other promotional items.

5. A library scavenger hunt (Goebel, Weingart, Johnson, & Dance, 2004) might help students feel more involved and provide an exciting game for them to investigate what the library has to offer.

6. If a library tour is not possible and if the librarian is giving a presentation to incoming students, it is best to keep moving and not remain standing still at the podium. Sitting in an auditorium for 45 minutes can be difficult for a student. Polger has noted that when he is constantly moving, students might be following him with their eyes. This might help prevent boredom as students might fall asleep if the presenter stands at the podium. The librarian providing the tours or giving the presentation might consider changing the inflections of his or her voice to avoid a monotone drone.

7. Providing multicolored handouts during library tours or during presentations provides a memorable, positive experience.

8. Providing short video clips (no longer than 1 minute) helps supplement the library tour or presentation.

9. If the librarian is providing a presentation using PowerPoint, it is best not to read the presentation since that represents poor presentation skills and that will affect student engagement. If the presenter is reading the PowerPoint slides, then there is no motivation to be engaged since the student could just as easily read the PowerPoint document at home. It is preferable to use PowerPoint as a visual aid and provide very little text. Reading the PowerPoint slides is also not advised since the presenter should be able to present the most important points without constantly referring to the slides. It also decreases engagement if the presenter does not face the audience and constantly reads the slides.

10. Gauge your audience: Morning library tours are easier to give since the members of the tour would be more awake and refreshed. Afternoon tours (given immediately after lunch) might mean sluggish, restless students. This means that the librarian providing an afternoon tour might have to be more energized and enthusiastic and to work harder.

11. Avoid using a script during a library tour. Every student group is different, and depending on how engaged they are, the presentation may have to be tweaked.

Targeting Specific Student Groups: Understanding Market Segmentation

Library instruction classes should be tailored and customized to a specific subgroup of the student population. If a student walks into the library instruction session and learns that it is a generic session with a librarian repeating the same concepts that he or she had already learned elsewhere, then it is likely that he or she will not be as engaged as the learner who attends a class that is customized to that person's learning and research needs. In order to successfully engage students, information literacy instruction must be promoted to specific groups (segments) of the college community (Venter, Wright, & Dibb, 2015). Those groups may include graduate students, first year students, international students, ELLs, honor students, students with disabilities, or even faculty. As an example, Polger teaches a first year college composition class very differently than a 400-level psychology class. When developing the lesson plan and handout, it is important to ensure the class and handout motivate students to use library resources.

Creating targeted classes is part of the academic librarian's mandate in order to best impart information literacy concepts to a specific class with a specific assignment. Targeting content helps engage students and motivates them to think of the library as a partner in their experiences as college students. Targeting specific student groups should also be part of the marketing process. The concept of targeting specific library users is known as market segmentation (Venter, Wright, & Dibb, 2015).

Segmenting users might help increase engagement because library users need to feel that they are not being overlooked. Among the typical library users (students, faculty, staff, alumni, and community), there are many subgroups and the marketing plan must meet the needs of all these users. The users also want to feel that their voices are being heard. For example, Polger's library offers specific new student orientation to nursing majors, honor students, international students, and student veterans.

Marketing First Year Library Workshops

Among the many teaching suggestions in library instruction design is the avoidance of library jargon (Freedman, 2015; Polger, 2011). In introducing the college library to students, part of the first year library workshop class must include promotional strategies to highlight both the facility (i.e., library building) and library services and resources (e.g., the website). Student engagement may increase if the librarian clearly indicates the purpose of the class, provides a basic outline of the workshop, and provides incentives. First year library workshops must promote what is considered appropriate for first year students: how to use your library card to get free things, how to find a textbook, how to borrow a laptop or calculator, and/or how to look up a book in the library catalog. In order to properly engage students, librarians must provide the tools for a gentle transition from high school to college. Librarians must be selective and not teach everything. First year students do not need to learn RefWorks but they should know what plagiarism is. Asking instructors who teach first year college students to provide the course syllabus and the assignment helps the librarian when developing an appropriate lesson plan. In conducting proper marketing research, librarians need to know in advance of the class sample topics to teach in order to understand what is trending and what is not. While global warming might be a popular topic in the news, legalization of marijuana might be more relevant to college students. If instructors do not give out research topics before the class, then gather a list of research topics students ask about at the reference desk. The information we receive at the reference desk can provide valuable data when teaching in the classroom.

First year students, in particular, might have library anxiety and be intimidated by the library (Jiao, Onwuegbuzie & Lichtenstein, 1996; Mech & Brooks, 1997; Mellon, 1986; Onwuegbuzie, Jiao, & Bostick, 2004). They might be hesitant to use library databases (and librarians cannot stop them from using Google) but librarians can make them feel more comfortable using the academic library and its resources.

Engagement is also connected with motivation. When students are motivated, this may lead to increased engagement (Saeed & Zyngier, 2012). According to the Encyclopedia of Education, "Motivation is also the study of what pushes or pulls an individual to start, direct, sustain, and finally end an activity" (Graham, Lepper, Henderlong, & Pintrich, 2002, p. 1690). Motivation is the emotional feeling that pushes you to complete a task for a specific reward. Engagement is deeper than motivation because it is a transformative experience that changes your attitude and behavior toward a specific issue (Marciano, 2011).

At Polger's institution, one of the major resources promoted in first year library workshops are textbooks used for courses. If students are motivated to succeed in class, they either purchase a textbook or borrow one from the library. Their decision to purchase or borrow a textbook might indicate their intention to succeed, possibly leading to an increased level of student engagement. At Polger's institution, the library promotes textbooks, group study rooms, and the website as the portal to access academic information for their courses. The liaison librarian model of service (Anderson & Puckett, 2014; Beasley & Rosseel, 2016) is also promoted so that students know that there is a subject specialist who is available to provide research assistance. Of course the liaison librarian model is promoted differently to faculty, since liaison librarians represent contact persons for collection decisions. Liaison librarians target specific academic departments with selective, curated promotional messages, e-mails, and promotional material in order to best engage their audience.

Teach to the Assignment

In the mind of a library marketer, information literacy instruction must be selective and targeted to a particular research assignment. Students and instructors feel that the class has greater value when it is tailored to a specific assignment. When librarians tailor classes, students and instructors feel they are being better served. To best tailor the class, librarians must collaborate with faculty in not only developing the lesson plan, but also developing proper assessment tools (Matthews & Chatterji, 2011; Rumble & Noe, 2009; Walker, 2008). There is a great deal of literature in support of the idea of librarian–faculty collaboration in developing effective and engaging library instruction (Black, Crest, & Volland, 2001; Carlson & Miller, 1984; Cunningham & Lanning, 2002; Gandhi, 2005; Ivey, 2003; Manuel, Beck, & Molloy, 2005; Reed, Kinder, & Farnum, 2007; Sanborn, 2005; Stein & Lamb, 1998). Engagement is limited due to the fact that many classes do not extend past the one-shot session. To better improve engagement, the authors feel that asking the instructor for a follow-up library instruction session might be beneficial to continue more hands-on learning. The authors believe that most students cannot retain selected information literacy concepts in a single lesson and therefore a second lesson might be helpful (Gandhi, 2005; Vossler & Sheidlower, 2011). In addition, repetition and review may help in the learning process. In the marketing plan for a college library's information literacy program, there should be a list of reasons as to why librarians should promote a follow-up session. The follow-up session does not improve student engagement but the opportunity of more hands-on learning time may contribute to an increase in student engagement. A marketing plan can also be used to document the steps involved in a class in order to ensure each library instruction session is a success.

Collaborating with Campus Departments

Librarians collaborate to get their message across and to raise the profile of their libraries to the larger college community. Librarians partner with faculty in the planning and delivery of library instruction sessions. In addition to collaborating with faculty, they also collaborate with campus departments to promote their information literacy programs. Campus-wide collaboration not only raises the awareness of the library to its stakeholders but also tries to build loyalty and advocates for the library. The authors reflect how their university (CUNY) promotes library partnerships with other campus departments.

Polger's library collaborates with the English department, the Registrar, college's writing center, academic support (tutoring office), new student programs office, LGBT resource center, and academic advising to promote information literacy classes to the college community. There is an abundance of literature that also discusses how college libraries partner with other campus units in order to promote information literacy (Gilman & Kunkel, 2010; Iannuzzi, 1998; Jacobson, 2001).

Marketing to International Students

To best serve international students, the library must ensure that international students are one of the segments that are recognized (Mu, 2007). Some libraries offer targeted classes that serve the needs of international students and students who are ELLs (Baron & Strout-Dapaz, 2001; Moeckel & Presnell, 1995). Library instructors must be aware of the issues facing international students, some which include loneliness, culture shock, language difficulties, difficulty adjusting to a new environment, and lack of basic library skills. Polger's library offers new student orientation and library workshops for introductory college composition classes tailored specifically to address the needs of international students. In order to best engage these students, librarians must use plain language, enunciate their words clearly, use repetition, speak slower than normal, use body language, and pay special attention to teaching plagiarism. They must avoid jargon, idioms, and colloquialisms (Mu, 2007). There is an extensive and growing existing literature on library services to international students (Allen, 1993; Amsberry, 2008, 2012; Badke, 2002; Baron & Strout-Dapaz, 2001; Curry & Copeman, 2005; Jackson, 2005; Liu, 1993; Natowitz, 1995; Patton, 2002). When developing information literacy classes for international students, plagiarism has been a problem with non-native English speakers (Badke, 2002; Hurley, Hegarty, & Bolger, 2006).

Wolfe (2005) discusses how international students can be targeted with various marketing initiatives. She specifically addresses creating a Web page (like a LibGuide) targeted at them, in addition to giving presentations, sending out communications, and promoting classes targeted at them. In Jackson's survey (2005), it was revealed that library tours for international students were an important vehicle in increasing student engagement, in addition to offering tailored classes that were appropriate for them. Kamhi-Stein and Stein (1998) suggest six principles when providing library instruction to international students. These principles are easy teaching techniques that can be used to increase engagement in the classroom. When students are more engaged, it is easier to promote different library services. Kamhi-Stein and Stein's (1998) six principles are as follows:

- slowing down speech and using repetition,
- engaging students by using learning activities that build upon each other,
- connecting topics in the library instruction class to the course content,
- remaining relevant to students' academic needs,
- integrating information competencies, and finally,
- incorporating hands-on activities.

Marketing to Graduate Students

Making assumptions about graduate students' information literacy skills can be dangerous. A graduate-level psychology class might have extensive experience using PsycINFO, writing research papers, or citing resources in APA (American Psychological Association) format but this might be vastly different from the graduate-level accounting class that has no experience with academic research, formulating a thesis statement, or creating a works-cited page. It is vital for the librarian to conduct preliminary research for the designated student segment and do a quick poll in the classroom to best understand how the librarian can meet the research needs of graduate students. Asking the professor in advance to poll their students to best understand their students' information literacy skills can help the librarian when developing the information literacy lesson.

For the last five years, Polger always gave a graduate-level information literacy one-shot class for graduate students in accounting. Each semester he asked the instructor to poll the students to understand how information literate the class was. It was surprising to learn that many of his accounting students had used the library to study but had never written a paper, nor conducted academic research. Although it was a graduate class, he felt that he had to treat the class like a 100-level freshman class since the students' information literacy skills are not strong enough.

Marketing to Faculty

Marketing to faculty must take into consideration their academic discipline, research interests, and level of teaching. In order to successfully engage faculty, librarians must communicate with classroom faculty and ask questions to get a sense of their research and teaching needs, so they can efficiently promote information literacy to them.

Polger engages the faculty he works with by providing constant communication before, during, and after the class. He provides feedback forms, quizzes, and pre- and posttests, as well as solicits anecdotal feedback from students and faculty. Each semester he sends out reminder e-mails and meets in person with selected faculty to ask them if would like to bring their class into the library. Making the in-person trips to their office, making individual "reminder" phone calls and sending individual e-mails show the classroom faculty member that Polger cares about the library instruction program and their classes. Polger targets his liaison subjects of English and psychology. In the past when he was the liaison to the chemistry and biology departments, he used to contact the instructors each semester and ask them if they were doing the same assignment with their learners. In addition, sending a message to the department secretaries and posting a flyer in the department also help gain exposure.

Each semester Polger's chief librarian holds meetings with each of the subject liaisons. In those meetings, she promotes library services and resources, as well as the liaison librarians who are the library contacts for each of the academic departments. If faculty have requests to order new books or consider subscriptions to specific academic journals, they can consult one of the liaison librarians. In addition to the chief's meetings, Polger makes a point of preparing welcome packages targeted to faculty. They include a library instruction brochure, a general brochure that focuses on library services, and a copy of the library newsletter (also targeted to faculty). Polger attaches his business card to the package and sends this to new faculty at the beginning of the fall semester as a way to welcome them to the library. The chief librarian also sends a message to all librarians with all the new hires each year. During the year, liaison librarians meet with classroom faculty and offer one-on-one instruction and formal faculty workshops. Most recently, the electronic resources librarian at Polger's CUNY college campus promoted subject-specific databases that could be used in specific classes. Once promoted, the liaison librarian works with the classroom faculty and may teach those databases in future library instruction classes.

When the college subscribed to the eMarketer database, Polger reached out to selected faculty in the marketing department and offered classes to marketing faculty and students. Another colleague created a marketing LibGuide following the launch of eMarketer, and Polger wrote a newsletter article promoting its launch. All these promotional initiatives were targeted primarily to marketing faculty.

Incorporating engagement (as a set of behaviors) in how information literacy is promoted is very important. Marketing cannot be completely successful without having an engaged audience. Librarians must assess how they promote information literacy by carefully curating how each academic department benefits from information literacy instruction.

As noted throughout this book, student engagement involves a combination of effective teaching practices, commonsense, strategic planning, patience, and a lot of creativity. Teaching is a skill that librarians continually need to sharpen. As teaching improves, engagement may improve. As learners become more engaged, they are motivated to learn more deeply and critically. There is no single way to successfully engage a single learner. Everyone learns differently, and the adventure is finding the best teaching method that helps the most learners connect. That "aha" moment is gratifying for both the learner and the instructor. The recipe for successful engagement occurs with the right combination of ingredients, gentle preparation, and experimenting with different herbs and spices, and then served with love.

Epilogue

As we wrap up this project that we started in the fall of 2014, we want to reflect on our experience in writing a book about teaching. We are inspired by the real teachers, the ones we had in elementary and high school. They are formally educated in teaching, and for the most part, they know "how" to teach. We were not trained as teachers.

We also wrote this book because we wanted to share a variety of teaching techniques to make learning fun and exciting. Over the last two years, we became immersed in the vast literature on student engagement. We learned that engagement is both a noun, verb, and adjective. For this book, we narrowed our focus to provide effective teaching techniques to engage students in an information literacy classroom.

When Scott and I graduated library school in 2000 from our prospective institutions (Queens College, City University of New York (CUNY), for Scott and the University of Western Ontario in London (Canada), for myself), we never imagined that classroom teaching was part of the librarian's portfolio of professional responsibilities. There were no classes in library school on pedagogy, or "how to teach." We never imagined having to "teach," let alone "engage," students in a classroom. At the time, we felt we were having an identity crisis. Were we librarians or teachers or both? What did it mean to be a "teacher" and what did it mean to "teach"?

When we started writing, we immediately saw how the book was taking shape. Our work represents the intersection of effective teaching methods and student engagement practices, all within the context of information literacy.

I was inspired by the two years of work that I did with my friend and colleague, Professor Karen Okamoto of John Jay College of Criminal Justice, CUNY. In May 2009, Karen and I presented at the Workshop on Instruction in Library Use (WILU) Conference in Montreal, Canada.

WILU is an information literacy conference and is known as "Canada's answer to Library Orientation Exchange (LOEX)"

The theme of the 2009 WILU Conference was "Reflections." Our presentation was entitled "Are Librarians Really Teachers?: Reflections and Analysis." Our presentation sparked an interest in us into thinking about whether librarians were teachers. Pauline Wilson certainly did not think we were teachers, as she indicated in her 1979 article "Librarians as Teachers: The Study of an Organization Fiction" (Wilson, 1979).

After the conference, Karen and I expanded our work into a peer-reviewed journal article entitled "Can't Anyone Be a Teacher Anyway?": Student Perceptions of Academic Librarians as Teachers," published in *Library Philosophy and Practice* in 2010. We both believed that teaching happens both in and out of the classroom and you do not need a teaching degree to "teach."

In 2012, Karen and I presented at the LOEX Conference in Columbus, Ohio. The theme was "E.A.T.: Energize, Accelerate, and Transform." The acronym was E.A.T. and many of the presentations were food themed. We presented on the practical tips used to engage students in the information literacy classroom. Our presentation was entitled "Blending, Mixing, and Processing: Strategies Used to Engage Students in the Classroom." It was at this conference that I noticed the word "engage" was becoming a buzzword. I initially assumed "engagement" was something symbolic that occurred before I got married over Labor Day weekend in 2011.

For the context of this book, Scott and I believe that engagement relates to the degree of commitment and connection to learning.

When Scott and I started working on this project, I must admit that it was a shift for me. Since most of my research falls within the scope of library marketing, I was apprehensive about starting a major project on a different topic. I consulted with Scott to work on this book because Scott also loves to teach and he had already coauthored a book in 2011 on humor and information literacy (with Joshua Vossler), *Humor and Information Literacy: Practical Techniques for Library Instruction.*

It was challenging to coauthor a book, let alone collaborate with a friend. Scott and I are not only close friends, but he fosters my two cats, and we have worked on several professional projects together over the last five years. Sometimes it can be difficult to work with a close friend who is also your colleague. We are also different in how we perform in our careers. I am an introvert who is terribly afraid of large groups. Scott, on the other hand, is a comedian both in his professional and in his personal life. He performs very well in front of a formal structured classroom setting.

Erving Goffman's dramaturgical techniques of front stage/back stage behavior (Goffman, 1959) best represent my teaching style. For me, teaching is a performance and not indicative of my authentic self. Students will often perceive me as extraverted, but they are surprised to learn when I tell them I am actually a painful introvert. They feel comfortable and unintimidated by my energy, my multicolored clothing and multicolored handouts and my teaching style, which, as noted throughout the book, involves constant dialogue, extreme energy, repetition, body movement, and playing with my voice intonations.

Scott and I have never worked in the same library together, yet we are employed in the same university system. One of the reasons is that we both work approximately 30 miles away from each other. For those of you who know New York City geography, I work in Staten Island and Scott works in Queens.

It was interesting and, for Scott, very educational to see and hear my thought processes and work processes. Scott learned a great deal about how I think and analyze ideas.

Scott's teaching style includes humor, as written throughout the book. The first day he taught in the Bushwick branch of the Brooklyn Public Library, he asked himself what did he want to happen. He realized he wanted students to walk out of the class remembering what he had taught them. He realized that the only thing he had remembered from eighth grade was a joke the teacher had told the class. Since he had decided that it worked as a pedagogical tool, he used it in the classroom. He found that it worked in the classroom and decided to use it as his favorite teaching tool. He has never been sorry, although some of his jokes are so poor, his students have been a bit aggrieved. On the other hand, these poor jokes means the students find him accessible and identify him as the librarian they want to speak with and work with. That makes him feel very proud, since he became a librarian to help students. This book was written to help the reader make such a connection with his or her patrons. If readers use those techniques in the book that appeal to them, then they will find that their patrons will be seeking them out to work with. If, on the other hand, someone became a librarian for the money, then they will be disappointed. We are not paid nearly enough, in Scott's opinion.

When I graduated from library school, I never imagined teaching in front of a class. In late 2001, I was asked to teach my very first library instruction class. I became very nervous. I thought I would freeze, pass out, or forget everything. Back then, we mostly used PowerPoint presentations as our teaching tool. In 2016, I would never use PowerPoint as I do not find it very engaging, especially when presenters read off their slides and turn their back on their students.

The only experience I had in public presentations was my experience working as a children's librarian in 2001 and 2002. I facilitated baby story time to a room full of two-year-olds. That was the scariest 30 minutes of my life trying to engage babies by reading them books, and singing lullabies. My supervisor encouraged me to further pursue children's librarianship since I had a "dynamic" personality, and at the time, it was rare to have male children's librarians, especially younger ones. I was flattered at the compliments, but I was determined to work in academic libraries.

In 2005, to supplement my full-time work, I pursued a part-time teaching opportunity at Seneca College in Toronto, Canada. I felt that teaching is best improved through practice. In 2006, I enrolled in Brock University's Bachelor of Education program in adult education. I already had a bachelor's degree and two master's degrees but felt that having an education degree would tie theory and practice together. I was fortunate that my employer (Humber River Hospital in Toronto, Canada) paid my tuition since my supervisor (who was not a librarian) believed that teaching was an integral part of the job.

I think I am a better teacher now than I was 12 years ago. I have taught "one-shot" workshops, full-semester courses, and half-semester courses. I have taught high school students, graduate students, physicians, nurses, medical residents, senior citizens, veterans, English language learners (ESL students), and library technician students.

Having worked in libraries in different capacities since 1988, I knew that I was entering a profession of service, of helping people, playing detective, and providing the highest quality information, all bundled in an organized fashion. Never did I imagine I would be teaching classes. I assumed the bulk of my job would be sitting at the reference desk.

Since starting at CUNY in 2008, I believe teaching represents 65 percent of my job, 25 percent marketing/outreach, 5 percent reference, 4 percent administrative duties, and 1 percent collection development. Scholarship does represent a large part of my role at CUNY, but librarians engage in scholarly research outside of our 35 hour workweek. Since teaching represents most of my job, I felt the need to contribute to the scholarship of teaching practice and teaching strategy.

In 2011 I started teaching part time at ASA College, where the college requires all first-year students to take a required two-credit information literacy class. I was excited to be able to have students for an entire semester. I went back to my CUNY college campus and asked many times if we could think about having a credit course in our department where we could teach students for an entire semester.

In the fall of 2014, the College of Staten Island Library offered its first credit-bearing information literacy course entitled "Beyond Google: Research for College Success." I was excited to be teaching this course both at my full-time job and at my part-time (evening/weekend) job. After teaching "Beyond Google" for several semesters, it officially became a regularized course in the college catalog in the fall of 2016.

Conclusion

Much of this book comes from our experiences in the trenches of the information literacy classroom. Since every academic institution has its own unique work culture, we decided to interview over 20 librarians who work in different and diverse academic settings. Our questionnaire had 900 respondents, which really opened our eyes on what student engagement means to librarians, the factors that influence engagement, and how we measure student engagement.

We have been very fortunate to work at two CUNY college campuses with thriving information literacy programs. Both our campuses believe that information literacy instruction is an important part of the college student's experience. We hope that this book inspires librarians to try different teaching methods and to experiment and leave their comfort zone. We have also learned that one technique might engage one student, while putting the other one to sleep. If we have put our entire class to sleep, we have learned not to take it personally. There are so many external factors that come into play that might affect the entire classroom dynamic.

Mark Aaron Polger

Appendix

Thank you for your interest in completing our questionnaire. We are seeking instruction librarians who provide one-shot instruction classes, who are embedded, or who teach "for credit" information literacy classes in academic institutions.

We are investigating the various teaching strategies you use in your classes to engage students. Student engagement can be a challenge for any educator. Many instruction librarians encounter obstacles when providing library instruction.

This activity has been reviewed and acknowledged by the CSI (City University of New York; College of Staten Island) Human Research Protection Program office.

Our questionnaire is voluntary and anonymous. There are no means of determining your name, e-mail address, or IP address. IP addresses are masked and data are anonymous.

You may withdraw from participating in this questionnaire at any time.

Consent: By completing the questionnaire, you are giving your consent to have your responses used in an accompanying study, which will be published by Libraries Unlimited/ABC-CLIO in 2017.

Contact: If you have any questions regarding your rights as a research subject, please contact the principal investigator at the e-mail below. Please feel free to forward the link to this questionnaire to your colleagues and friends!

Thanks so much,

Mark Aaron Polger, Principal Investigator
Assistant Professor and First Year Experience Librarian
College of Staten Island Library, City University of New York
MarkAaron.Polger@csi.cuny.edu
718–982–4065

1. What type of academic library do you work?

   A. Private two-year college
   B. Private four-year college
   C. Public two-year college
   D. Public four-year college
   E. Other _______

2. Age category (not mandatory)

   A. 18–30
   B. 31–40
   C. 41–50
   D. 51–60
   E. 61–70
   F. 71+

3. What model of library instruction do you teach? (*You may select more than one response.*)

   A. I teach one-shot library instruction sessions.
   B. I teach both one-shot and "for-credit" classes.
   C. I teach "credit-bearing" classes.
   D. I am embedded over a longer period of time.
   E. I teach "one-shot" library instruction online.
   F. I teach "for-credit" library instruction online.
   G. Other (please specify):

4. Please check off the keywords that describe "student engagement" to you. Please check off as many keywords as you like. They are listed in alphabetical order for your convenience.

   A. Attention
   B. Belong
   C. Bridge
   D. Care
   E. Connect
   F. Converse
   G. Curiosity
   H. Dialogue
   I. Discuss
   J. Energize
   K. Exchange
   L. Grow
   M. Inspire
   N. Interact

    O. Interest
    P. Invigorate
    Q. Involve
    R. Learn
    S. Motivate
    T. Passion
    U. Refresh
    V. Revitalize
    W. Share
    X. Other (please specify):_______

5. How do you perceive students' feelings as you begin a library instruction session? (*You may select more than one response.*)

    A. Students appear excited.
    B. Students are open-minded.
    C. Students are apathetic.
    D. Students look bored.
    E. Students look unhappy.
    F. I am unsure.

6. What techniques do you use to engage students during classes?

    A. Role-play
    B. Humor
    C. Body movements
    D. Theatrics
    E. Storytelling
    F. "Real-world" examples
    G. Class activities
    H. Instructional scaffolding
    I. Multimedia (YouTube videos)
    J. Dialogue/discussion
    K. Other (please specify):_______

7. How do you assess if you have successfully engaged students during your class?

    A. Pretest (quiz)
    B. Posttest (quiz)
    C. Survey
    D. In-person interviews/consultations
    E. Feedback form
    F. Observational data
    G. In-class exercises
    H. Other (please specify):_______

8.   Based on the following engagement techniques, please rank how effective
     each strategy is.

	Very Engaging	**Somewhat Engaging**	**Not Very Engaging**	**Not Engaging**
Tailoring a class				
Tailoring a handout				
Humor				
Storytelling				
Real-world examples				
Role-play/games				
Clickers				
Theatrics				
Multimedia				
Hands-on time (learning by doing)				

9.   Check the following factors that might influence student engagement.

     A.   "One-shot" versus "for-credit" classes
     B.   Embedded librarian
     C.   Classroom space
     D.   Classroom location
     E.   Disruptive students
     F.   Disinterested faculty
     G.   Technology
     H.   Time of the day
     I.   Weather
     J.   Discipline
     K.   Level of class (undergraduate or graduate level)
     L.   Number of library instruction classes a student has already attended
     M.   Other (please specify): _______

10. Additional comments?

____

____

References

Adcox, S. (2015, October 6). *Who are the baby boomers?: Early boomers, late boomers can be very different.* Retrieved from http://grandparents.about.com/od/grandparentsglossary/g/Baby-Boomers-Who-Are-The-Baby-Boomers.htm

Adler, K. (2013). Radical purpose: The critical reference dialogue at a progressive urban college. *Urban Library Journal, 19*(1), 1–8. Retrieved from http://ojs.gc.cuny.edu/index. php/urbanlibrary/article/view/1395

Allen, M. B. (1993). International students in academic libraries: A user survey, *College & Research Libraries, 54*(4), 323–333. doi:10.5860/crl_54_04_323

American Library Association. (1996). *Library bill of rights.* Retrieved from http://www.ala.org/advocacy/intfreedom/librarybill

American Library Association. (2008, January 22). B.1 core values, ethics, and core competencies (old number 40). Retrieved January 10, 2016, from B.1.2 Code of professional ethics for librarians (old number 40.2) Web site: http://www.ala.org/aboutala/governance/policymanual/updatedpolicymanual/section2/4 corevalues

American Library Association, Association of College and Research Libraries. (2000). *Information literacy competency standards for higher education.* Retrieved from http://www.ala.org/acrl/standards/informationliteracycompetency

American Library Association, Association of College and Research Libraries. (2015). *Framework for information literacy for higher education.* Retrieved from http://acrl.ala.org/ilstandards/wp-content/uploads/2015/01/Framework-MW15-Board Docs.pdf

American Library Association, Association of College and Research Libraries, Presidential Committee on Information Literacy. (1989). *Final report.* Retrieved from http://www.ala.org/acrl/publications/whitepapers/presidential

American Marketing Association. (2013). *Approved definition of marketing by the AMA board of directors.* Retrieved from https://www.ama.org/AboutAMA/Pages/Definition-of-Marketing.aspx

Amsberry, D. (2008). Talking the talk: library classroom communication and international students. *Journal of Academic Librarianship, 34*(4), 354–357. doi:10.1016/j.acalib.2008.05.007

Amsberry, D. (2012). Engaging international students with the academic library. In L. Snavely (Ed.). *Student engagement and the academic library* (pp. 71–83). Santa Barbara, CA: Libraries Unlimited.

Anderson, J. E., & Puckett, J. (2014). Crossing disciplines, creating space: Using drop-in research labs to support an interdisciplinary research-intensive capstone course. *Practical Academic Librarianship: The International Journal of the SLA Academic Division, 4*(1), 1–14.

Andreola, B. (2012). Engagement (Engajamento). In *Paulo Freire Encyclopedia* (pp. 122–124). Lanham, MD: Rowman & Littlefield.

Arnold-Garza, S. (2014). The flipped classroom: Assessing an innovative teaching model for effective and engaging library instruction. *College & Research Libraries News, 75*(1), 10–13.

Arnsan, D. (2000). Libraries, laughter and learning: The rubber chicken school of bibliographic instruction. *Community & Junior College Libraries, 9*(4), 53–58. doi:10.1300/J107v09n04_07

Ash, K. (2012, August 29). Educators evaluate "flipped classrooms": Benefits and drawbacks seen in replacing lectures with on-demand video. *Education Week, 32*(2), s6. Retrieved from http://go.galegroup.com/ps/i.do?id=GALE %7CA301921221&v=2.1&u=cuny_statenisl &it=r&p=AONE&sw=w&a sid=16fff1fc159a8d733844d920f0947335

Badke, W. (2002). International students: Information literacy or academic literacy? *Academic Exchange Quarterly, 6*(4), 60.

Banks, J., & Pracht, C. (2008). Reference desk staffing trends: A survey. *Reference & User Services Quarterly, 48*(1), 54–59. doi:10.5860/rusq.48n1.54

Barkley, E. F. (2010). *Student engagement techniques: A handbook for college faculty.* San Francisco, CA: Jossey-Bass.

Baron, S., & Strout-Dapaz, A. (2001). Communicating with and empowering international students with a library skills set. *Reference Services Review, 29*(4), 314–326. doi:10.1108/00907320110408447

Battleson, B., Booth, A., & Weintrop, J. (2001). Usability testing of an academic library web site: A case study. *The Journal of Academic Librarianship, 27*(3), 188–198. doi:10.1016/S0099–1333(01)00180-X

Bean, T. M., & Thomas, S. N. (2010). Being like both: Library instruction methods that outshine the one-shot. *Public Services Quarterly, 6*(2/3), 237–249. doi: 10.1080/15228959.2010.497746

Beasley, G., & Rosseel, T. (2016). Leaning into sustainability at University of Alberta Libraries. *Library Management, 37*(3), 136–148. doi:10.1108/ LM-04–2016–0023

Beck, S. E., & Turner, N. B. (2001). On the fly BI: Reaching and teaching from the reference desk. *The Reference Librarian, 34*(72), 83–96. doi:10.1300/ J120v34n72_08

Behrens, S. J. (1994). A conceptual analysis and historical overview of information literacy. *College and Research Libraries, 55*(4), 309–322. doi:10.5860/ crl_55_04_309

Bell, A. (2013). Paws for a study break: Running an animal-assisted therapy program at the Gerstein Science Information Centre. *Partnership: The Canadian Journal of Library and Information Practice and Research, 8*(1), 1–14. doi:10.21083/partnership.v8i1.2403

Bell, S. (2008). Keeping them enrolled: How academic libraries contribute to student retention. *Library Issues, 29*(1), 1–4.

Benefiel, C. R., Arant, W., & Gass, E. (1999). A new dialogue: A student advisory committee in an academic library. *The Journal of Academic Librarianship, 25*(2), 111–113. doi:10.1016/S0099–1333(99)80008–1

Berger, K. W., & Hines, R. W. (1994). What does the user really want? The library user survey project at Duke University. *The Journal of Academic Librarianship, 20*(5), 306–309. doi:10.1016/0099–1333(94)90068–X

Berk, R. A. (2002). *Humor as an instructional defibrillator: Evidence-based techniques in teaching and assessment.* Sterling, VA: Stylus.

Berk, R. A. (2003). *Professors are from Mars, students are from Snickers: How to write and deliver humor in the classroom and in professional presentations.* Sterling, VA: Stylus.

Biggs, M. (1981). Sources of tension and conflict between librarians and faculty. *The Journal of Higher Education, 52*(2), 182–201 doi: 10.2307/1981090

Black, C., Crest, S., & Volland, M. (2001). Building a successful information literacy infrastructure on the foundation of librarian–faculty collaboration. *Research Strategies, 18*(3), 215–225. doi:10.1016/S0734–3310(02)00085–X

Black, S. (2003). Engaging the Disengaged. *American School Board Journal, 190*(12), 58.

Bloom, B. S. (1956). *Taxonomy of educational objectives; The classification of educational goals.* New York, NY: McKay.

Blummer, B. A., & Kritskaya, O. (2009). Best practices for creating an online tutorial: A literature review. *Journal of Web Librarianship, 3*(3), 199–216. doi:10.1080/19322900903050799

Bonn, G. S. (1974). Evaluation of the collection. *Library Trends, 22*(3), 265–304.

Bosman, E., & Rusinek, C. (1997). Creating the user-friendly library by evaluating patron perception of signage. *Reference Services Review, 25*(1), 71–82. doi:10.1108/00907329710306599

Bowles-Terry, M., Hensley, M. K., & Hinchliffe, L. J. (2010). Best practices for online video tutorials: A study of student preferences and understanding. *Communications in Information Literacy, 4*(1), 17–28 Retrieved from http://www.comminfolit.org/index.php/cil/article/view/Vol4-2010AR1

Brannon, S. (2010). SMS reference. *The Reference Librarian, 52*(1/2), 152–158. doi:10.1080/02763877.2011.523817

Branon, R. F., & Essex, C. (2001). Synchronous and asynchronous communication tools in distance education. *TechTrends, 45*(1), 36–36. doi:10.1007/BF02763377

Brinthaupt, T. M., Fisher, L. S., Gardner, J. G., Raffo, D. M., & Woodard, J. B. (2011). What the best online teachers should do. *Journal of Online Learning and Teaching, 7*(4), 515–524.

Brock, S., & Tabaei, S. (2011). Library and marketing class collaborate to create next generation learning landscape. *Reference Services Review, 39*(3), 362–368. doi:10.1108/00907321111161377

Brooks, M., & Zubarev, M. (2012). Another lane on the information highway? A case study of experimenting with text message reference. *The Reference Librarian, 53*(2), 170–181.

Burhanna, K. J., Eschedor Voelker, T. J., & Gedeon, J. A. (2008). Virtually the same: Comparing the effectiveness of online versus in-person library tours. *Public Services Quarterly, 4*(4), 317–338. doi:10.1080/15228950802461616

Carlson, D., & Miller, R. H. (1984). Librarians and teaching faculty: Partners in bibliographic instruction. *College and Research Libraries, 45*(6), 483–91. doi:10.5860/crl_45_06_483

Carlson, S. (2007). Are reference desks dying out? Librarians struggle to redefine—and in some cases eliminate—the venerable institution. *The Reference Librarian, 48*(2), 25–30. doi:10.1300/J120v48n02_06

Cassidy, E. D., Colmenares, A., & Martinez, M. (2014). So text me—Maybe. *Reference & User Services Quarterly, 53*(4), 300–312.

Center for Applied Special Technology. (2011). Universal Design for Learning Guidelines. Retrieved from http://www.udlcenter.org/sites/udlcenter.org/files/updateguidelines2_0.pdf

Chapman, A. J., & Crompton, P. (1988). Humorous presentations of material and presentations of humorous material: A review of the humour and memory literature and two experimental studies. In M. M. Gruneberg, P. E. Morris, & R. N. Sykes (Eds.), *Practical aspects of memory* (pp. 84–92). London, United Kingdom: Academic Press.

Chapman, S., & Cantrell, P. (2016). What is an Instructional Designer? In *Teaching at Colorado State University*. Retrieved from http://teaching.colostate.edu/tips/tip.cfm?tipid=70

Charnigo, L. (2009). Lights! camera! action! Producing library instruction video tutorials using Camtasia Studio. *Journal of Library & Information Services in Distance Learning, 3*(1), 23–30. doi:10.1080/15332900902794880

Chen, P. S. D., Lambert, A. D., & Guidry, K. R. (2010). Engaging online learners: The impact of web-based learning technology on college student engagement. *Computers & Education, 54*(4), 1222–1232. doi:10.1016/j.compedu.2009.11.008

Chernow, R. (2005). *Alexander Hamilton.* New York, NY: Penguin.

Chesnut, S. (1998). Queering the curriculum or what's Walt Whitman got to do with it? In R. L. Sanlo (Ed.), *Working with lesbian, gay, bisexual, and transgender college students: A handbook for faculty and administrators* (pp. 223–230). Westport, CT: Greenwood.

Chickering, A. W., & Gamson, Z. F. (1987). *Seven principles for good practice in under-graduate education.* Retrieved from http://teaching.uncc.edu/learning-resources/articles-books/best-practice/education-philosophy/seven-principles

Chodock, T., & Dolinger, E. (2009). Applying universal design to information literacy: Teaching students who learn differently at Landmark College. *Reference & User Services Quarterly, 49*(1), 24–32.

Churkovich, M., & Oughtred, C. (2002). Can an online tutorial pass the test for library instruction? An evaluation and comparison of library skills instruction methods for first year students at Deakin University. *Australian Academic & Research Libraries, 33*(1), 25–38. doi:10.1080/00048623.2002.10755177

Clark, W. S., & Wallin, C. (1999). Faculty response to library technology: Insights on attitudes. *Library Trends, 47*(4), 640–668.

Cohen, M. E. (2016). The flipped classroom as a tool for engaging discipline faculty in collaboration: A case study in library-business collaboration. *New Review of Academic Librarianship, 22*(1), 5–23.

Cohen, M. E., Lehner-Quam, A., Poggiali, J., & Wright, R. (2016). A study of flipped information literacy sessions for business management and education. *CUNY Academic Works*. Retrieved from http://academicworks.cuny.edu/le_pubs/161

Cole, V., & Krkoska, B. B. (2010). Launching a text a librarian service: Cornell's preliminary experiences. *The Reference Librarian, 52*(1/2), 3–8. doi:10.1080/02763877.2011.521881

Coonin, B. C., & Levine, C. (2013). Reference interviews: Getting things right. *The Reference Librarian, 54*(1), 73–77, doi:10.1080/02763877.2013.735578

Costello, B., Lenholt, R., & Stryker, J. (2004). Using Blackboard in library instruction: Addressing the learning styles of Generations X and Y. *The Journal of Academic Librarianship, 30*(6), 452–460. doi:10.1016/j.acalib.2004.07.003

Cothran, D. J., Pamela, H. K., Banville, D., Choi, E., Amade-Escot, C., MacPhail, A., . . . Kirk, D. (2005). A cross-cultural investigation of the use of teaching styles. *Research Quarterly for Exercise and Sport, 76*(2), 193–201. Retrieved from http://york.ezproxy.cuny.edu:2048/login?url=http://search.proquest.com/docview/21854330?accountid=15180

Crowley, G. H., Leffel, R., Ramirez, D., Hart, J. L., & Armstrong, T. S. (2002). User perceptions of the library's web pages: A focus group study at Texas A&M University. *The Journal of Academic Librarianship, 28*(4), 205–210. doi:10.1016/S0099–1333(02)00284–7

Cunningham, T. H., & Lanning, S. (2002). New frontier trail guides: Faculty-librarian collaboration on information literacy. *Reference Services Review, 30*(4), 343–348. doi:10.1108/00907320210451349

Curry, A., & Copeman, D. (2005). Reference service to international students: A field stimulation research study. *The Journal of Academic Librarianship, 31*(5), 409–420. doi:10.1016/j.acalib.2005.05.011

Darby, A. (n.d.). *Understanding universal design in the classroom*. Retrieved from http://www.nea.org/home/34693.htm

Datig, I., & Ruswick, C. (2013). Four quick flips activities for the information literacy classroom. *College & Research Libraries News, 74*(5), 249–257.

Daugherty, T. K., & Carter, E. W. (1997). Assessment of outcome-focused library instruction in psychology. *Journal of Instructional Psychology, 24*(1), 29.

Davis, D. M. (2009). *Planning for 2015: The recent history and future supply of librarians.* Retrieved from http://www.ala.org/research/sites/ala.org.research/files/content/librarystaffstats/recruitment/Librarians_supply_demog_analys.pdf

Davis, K. (2008). Intersectionality as buzzword: A sociology of science perspective on what makes a feminist theory successful. *Feminist Theory, 9*(1), 67–85. doi:10.1177/1464700108086364

Davis, A. L. (2013). Using instructional design principles to develop effective information literacy instruction: The ADDIE model. *College & Research Libraries News, 74*(4), 205–207.

Denda, K. (2015). Developing interview skills and visual literacy: A new model of engagement for academic libraries. *Portal: Libraries and the Academy, 15*(2), 299–314. doi:10.1353/pla.2015.0024

Department of Natural and Cultural Resources, North Carolina Arts Council, A+ Schools Program. (n.d.). *Howard Gardner's theory of multiple intelligences.* Retrieved from http://www.uncg.edu/aps/multipleintelligences.pdf

Desai, C. M., & Graves, S. J. (2008). Cyberspace or face-to-face: The teachable moment and changing reference mediums. *Reference & User Services Quarterly, 47*(3), 242–255. doi:10.5860/rusq.47n3.242

Deuink, A. L., & Seiler, M. (2006). Students as library advocates The library student advisory board at Pennsylvania State-Schuylkill. *College & Research Libraries News, 67*(1), 18–21.

Deuink, A. L., & Seiler, M. (2009). *The library student advisory board: Why your academic library needs it and how to make it work.* Jefferson, NC: McFarland.

Dewald, N. H. (1999). Transporting good library instruction practices into the web environment: An analysis of online tutorials. *The Journal of Academic Librarianship, 25*(1), 26–31. doi:10.1016/S0099–1333(99)80172–4

Dill, E. (2008). Do clickers improve library instruction? Lock in your answers now. *The Journal of Academic Librarianship, 34*(6), 527–529. doi:10.1016/j.acalib.2008.09.004

Dixson, M. D. (2012). Creating effective student engagement in online courses: What do students find engaging? *Journal of the Scholarship of Teaching and Learning, 10*(2), 1–13.

Duggan, M., & Rainie, L. (2012, November 25). *Cell phone activities 2012.* Retrieved from http://www.pewinternet.org/2012/11/25/cell-phone-activities-2012/

Educause Learning Initiative (2006, May). *7 things you should know about google jockeying.* Retrieved from https://net.educause.edu/ir/library/pdf/ELI7014.pdf

Educause Learning Initiative (2012, February). *7 things you should know about flipped classrooms.* Retrieved from https://net.educause.edu/ir/library/pdf/ELI7081.pdf

Edutainment. (n.d.). In *Merriam-Webster Dictionary.* Retrieved from http://www.merriam-webster.com/dictionary/edutainment

Eisner, E. W. (2000). Benjamin Bloom. *Prospects, 30*(3), 387–395. doi:10.1007/BF02754061

Elmborg, J. K. (2002). Teaching at the desk: Toward a reference pedagogy. *Portal: Libraries and the Academy, 2*(3), 455–464. doi:10.1353/pla.2002.0050

Emdin, C. (2016). *For white folks who teach in the hood . . . and the rest of y'all too: Reality pedagogy and urban education.* Boston, MA: Beacon.

Evans, G. E. (1970). Book selection and book collection usage in academic libraries. *The Library Quarterly, 40*(3), 297–308. doi:10.1086/619865

Fagan-Wilen, R., Springer, D. W., Ambrosino, B., & White, B. W. (2006). The support of adjunct faculty: An academic imperative. *Social Work Education, 25*(1), 39–51. doi:10.1080/02615470500477870

Farmer, H., McKay, R., & Tsakiris, M. (2014). Trust in me: Trustworthy others are seen as more physically similar to the self. *Psychological Science, 25*(1), 290–292. doi:10.1177/0956797613494852

Ferguson, C. D., & Bunge, C. A. (1997). The shape of services to come: Values-based reference service for the largely digital library. *College & Research Libraries, 58*(3), 252–265. doi:10.5860/crl.58.3.252

Fine, L. E. (2011). Minimizing heterosexism and homophobia: Constructing meaning of out campus LGB life. *Journal of Homosexuality, 58*(4), 521–546. doi:10.1080/00918369.2011.555673

Flaspohler, M. R. (2012). *Engaging first year students in meaningful library research: A practical guide for teaching faculty.* Oxford, UK: Chandos.

Foster, A. L. (2008, April 18). Snacks in the stacks: Libraries welcome food amid the books. *Chronicle of Higher Education.* Retrieved from http://chronicle.com/article/Snacks-in-the-Stacks-/34823

Freedman, K. (2015). Library instruction design: Learning from Google and Apple (Chandos Information Professional Series). *The Australian Library Journal, 64*(3), 245–246. doi:10.1080/00049670.2015.1048568

Fried, C. B. (2008). In-class laptop use and its effects on student learning. *Computers & Education, 50*(3), 906–914. doi:10.1016/j.compedu.2006.09.006

Fromm, J., & Garton, C. (2013). *Marketing to millennials: Reach the largest and most influential generation of consumers ever.* New York, NY: AMA.

Frymier, A. B., & Weser, B. (2001). The role of student dispositions on student expectations for instructor communication behavior. *Communication Education, 50*(4), 314–326. doi:10.1080/03634520109379258

Galvin, J. (2006). Information literacy and integrative learning. *College & Undergraduate Libraries, 13*(3), 25–51. doi:10.1300/J106v13n03_03

Gandhi, S. (2005). Faculty-librarian collaboration to assess the effectiveness of a five-session library instruction model. *Community & Junior College Libraries, 12*(4), 15–48. doi:10.1300/J107v12n04_05

Gardner, H. (1983). *Frames of mind: The theory of multiple intelligences.* New York, NY: Basic Books.

Gervasio, D. I. (2014). Redefining virtual: Leveraging mobile librarians for SMS reference. *International Journal of Digital Library Systems, 4*(2), 44–69. doi:10.4018/IJDLS.2014070104

Gibson, C., Ed. (2006). *Student engagement and information literacy.* Chicago, IL: Association of College and Research Libraries.

Gibson, S. E. (2009). Enhancing intergenerational communication in the classroom: Recommendations for successful teacher–student relationships. *Nursing Education Perspectives, 30*(1), 37–39.

Gilman, I., & Kunkel, M. (2010). From passive to pervasive: Changing perceptions of the library's role through intra-campus partnerships. *Collaborative Leadership, 2*(1), 22–32.

Girven, W. (2012). Invisible connections: Creating community through oral storytelling in the UAS listening project. In L. Snavely (Ed.), *Student engagement and the academic library* (pp. 1–10). Santa Barbara, CA: Libraries Unlimited.

Goffman, E. (1959). *The presentation of self in everyday life.* New York, NY: Random House.

Gough, C., & Greenblatt, E. (Eds.). (1990). *Gay and lesbian library service.* Jefferson, NC: McFarland.

Goebel Brown, A., Weingart, S., Johnson, J. R., & Dance, B. (2004). Librarians don't bite: Assessing library orientation for freshmen. *Reference Services Review, 32*(4), 394–403. doi:10.1108/00907320410569752

Graham, S., Lepper, M. R., Henderlong, J., & Pintrich, P. R. (2002). Motivation. In J. W. Guthrie (Ed.), *Encyclopedia of Education* (2nd ed., Vol. 5, pp. 1690–1701). New York, NY: Macmillan Reference USA. Retrieved from http://go.galegroup.com

Grassian, E. S., & Kaplowitz, J. R. (2001). *Information literacy instruction: Theory and practice. Information literacy sourcebooks.* Edison, NJ: Neal-Schuman.

Grassian, E., & Trueman, R. B. (2007). Stumbling, bumbling, teleporting and flying. . . librarian avatars in Second Life. *Reference Services Review, 35*(1), 84–89.

Grider, S. (1995). Passed down from generation to generation: Folklore and teaching. *The Journal of American Folklore, 108*(428), 178–185. doi:10.2307/541378

Gupta, V. (2015, May 27). Celebrating access today: 25th anniversary year of the Americans with Disabilities Act. [Web log]. Retrieved from http://www.justice.gov/opa/blog/celebrating-access-today-25th-anniversary-year-americans-disabilities-act-3

Haddow, G., & Joseph, J. (2010). Loans, logins, and lasting the course: Academic library use and student retention. *Australian Academic & Research Libraries, 41*(4), 233–244. doi:10.1080/00048623.2010.10721478

Hagopian, K. J. (2013) Rethinking the structural architecture of the college classroom. *New Directions for Teaching and Learning, 2013*(135), 7–18. doi:10.1002/tl.20059

Hall, T., & Martin, B. (2013). Engagement of African-American college students through the use of hip hop pedagogy. *International Journal of Pedagogies and Learning, 8*(2), 93–105. doi:10.5172/rjpl.2013.8.2.93

Hamilton. An American musical. (n.d.). *Cast and creative: Lin-Manuel Miranda.* Retrieved May 2, 2015, from http://www.hamiltonbroadway.com/cast.php

Hands, A. S. (2015). *Successfully serving the college bound.* Chicago, IL: ALA Editions.

Hill, J. B., Hill, C. M., & Sherman, D. (2007). Text messaging in an academic library: Integrating SMS into digital reference. *The Reference Librarian, 47*(1), 17–29.

Hiller, S. (2001). Assessing user needs, satisfaction, and library performance at the University of Washington Libraries. *Library Trends, 49*(4), 605.

Höglund, E. (2014). Focus groups—Stimulating and rewarding co-operation between the library and its patrons. *Qualitative & Quantitative Methods in Libraries,* (2), 425–431.

hooks, B. (1994). *Teaching to transgress: Education as the practice of freedom.* New York, NY: Routledge.

Hoover, E. (2009, October 11). The millennial muddle: How stereotyping students became a thriving industry and a bundle of contradictions. *The Chronicle of Higher Education.* Retrieved from http://chronicle.com/article/The-Millennial-Muddle-How/48772/

Hopkins, F. L. (1982). A century of bibliographic instruction: The historical claim to professional and academic legitimacy. *College and Research Libraries, 43*(3), 192–198. doi:10.5860/crl_43_03_192

Hoppenfeld, J. (2012). Keeping students engaged with web-based polling in the library instruction session. *Library Hi Tech, 30*(2), 235–252. doi:10.1108/07378831211239933

Howe, N., & Strauss, W. (2000). *Millennials rising: The next great generation.* New York, NY: Vintage.

Hoyt, J. E. (2012). Predicting the satisfaction and loyalty of adjunct faculty. *The Journal of Continuing Higher Education, 60*(3), 132–142. doi:10.1080/07377363.2013.722417

Hrastinski, S. (2008). Asynchronous and synchronous e-learning. *Educause Quarterly, 31*(4), 51–55.

Hurley, T., Hegarty, N., & Bolger, J. (2006). Crossing a bridge: The challenges of developing and delivering a pilot information literacy course for international students. *New Library World, 107*(7/8), 302–320. doi:10.1108/03074800610677281

Iannuzzi, P. (1998). Faculty development and information literacy: Establishing campus partnerships. *Reference Services Review, 26*(3/4), 97–102. doi:10.1108/00907329810307786

Ivey, R. (2003). Information literacy: How do librarians and academics work in partnership to deliver effective learning programs? *Australian Academic & Research Libraries, 34*(2), 100–113. doi:10.1080/00048623.2003.10755225

Jackson, P. A. (2005). Incoming international students and the library: A survey. *Reference Services Review, 33*(2), 197–209. doi:10.1108/00907320510597408

Jackson, P. A. (2007). Integrating information literacy into Blackboard: Building campus partnerships for successful student learning. *The Journal of Academic Librarianship, 33*(4), 454–461.

Jacobson, T. E. (2001). Partnerships between library instruction units and campus teaching centers. *The Journal of Academic Librarianship, 27*(4), 311–316. doi:10.1016/S0099-1333(01)00217-8

Jaguszewski, J., & Williams, K. (2013). *New roles for new times: Transforming liaison roles in research libraries.* Washington, DC: Association of Research Libraries.

Jiao, Q. G., Onwuegbuzie, A. J., & Lichtenstein, A. A. (1996). Library anxiety: Characteristics of "at-risk" college students. *Library & Information Science Research, 18*(2), 151–163. doi:10.1016/S0740-8188(96)90017-1

Johnson, D. I. (2013). Student in-class texting behavior: Associations with instructor clarity and classroom relationships. *Communication Research Reports, 30*(1), 57–62. doi:10.1080/08824096.2012.723645

Julien, H., & Given, L. M. (2003). Faculty–librarian relationships in the information literacy context: A content analysis of librarians' expressed attitudes and experiences. *Canadian Journal of Information and Library Science, 27*(3), 65–88.

Kamhi-Stein, L. D., & Stein, A. P. (1998). Teaching information competency as a third language: A new model for library instruction. *Reference & User Services Quarterly,* 173–179.

Kaplan, R. M., & Pascoe, G. C. (1977). Humorous lectures and humorous examples: Some effects upon comprehension and retention. *Journal of Educational Psychology, 69*(1), 61–65. doi:10.1037/0022-0663.69.1.61

Karle, E. M. (2008). Invigorating the academic library experience creative programming ideas. *College & Research Libraries News, 69*(3), 141–144.

Kaser, D. (1982). Standards for college libraries. *Library Trends, 31*(1), 7–19.

Kendall, T. (2016, March 14). "Hamilton" cast, NYC public school students at White House to promote history, the arts. *New York Daily News.* Retrieved from http://www.nydailynews.com/entertainment/theater-arts/amilton-cast-nyc-students-promote-history-white-house-article-1.2564443

Kersten, D. (2002). Today's generations face new communication gaps. Retrieved October 20, 2016, from http://www.usatoday.com/money/jobcenter/workplace/communications/2002

Kim, M. K., Kim, S. M., Khera, O., & Getman, J. (2014). The experience of three flipped classrooms in an urban university: An exploration of design principles. *The Internet and Higher Education, 22,* 37–50. doi:10.1016/j.iheduc.2014.04.003

Kincheloe, J. L. (2004). *Critical pedagogy primer.* New York, NY: Peter Lang. Retrieved from http://www.ebrary.com

Kingsbury, M. (2015). How to smile when they can't see your face: Rhetorical listening strategies for IM and SMS reference. *International Journal of Digital Library Systems, 5*(1), 31–44. doi:10.4018/IJDLS.2015010104

Knapp, A. E. (2004). We asked them what they thought, now what do we do? The use of LibQUAL+ data to redesign public services at the University of Pittsburgh. *Journal of Library Administration, 40*(3/4), 157–171. doi:10.1300/J111v40n03_12

Kniffel, L. (1999). Gay liberation: From task force to round table. *American Libraries, 30*(11), 74.

Kolb, A. Y., & Kolb, D. A. (2005). Learning styles and learning spaces: Enhancing experiential learning in higher education. *Academy of Management Learning & Education, 4*(2), 193–212. doi:10.5465/AMLE.2005.17268566

Kolb, D. A. (2014). *Experiential learning: Experience as the source of learning and development* (2nd ed.). Indianapolis, IN: FT Press.

Kong, S. C. (2014). Developing information literacy and critical thinking skills through domain knowledge learning in digital classrooms: An experience of practicing flipped classroom strategy. *Computers & Education, 78,* 160–173. doi:10.1016/j.compedu.2014.05.009

Korobkin, D. (1988). Humor in the classroom: Considerations and strategies. *Classroom Teaching, 36*(1), 154–158. Retrieved from http://heldref.metapress.com/app/home/journal.asp?referrer=parent&backto=subject,4,13

Koshik, I., & Okazawa, H. (2012). A conversation analytic study of actual and potential problems in communication in library chat reference interactions. *Journal of the American Society for Information Science and Technology, 63*(10), 2006–2019. doi:10.1002/asi.22677

Kotter, W. R. (1999). Bridging the great divide: Improving relations between librarians and classroom faculty. *The Journal of Academic Librarianship, 25*(4), 294–303. doi:10.1016/S0099–1333(99)80030–5

Kuh, G. D. (2001). Assessing what really matters to student learning: Inside the national survey of student engagement. *Change: The Magazine of Higher Learning, 33*(3), 10–17. doi:10.1080/00091380109601795

Kuh, G. D. (2008) *High-impact educational practices: A brief overview.* Retrieved from https://www.aacu.org/leap/hips

Kuh, G. D., & Gonyea, R. M. (2003). The role of the academic library in promoting student engagement in learning. *College & Research Libraries, 64*(4), 256–282. doi:10.5860/crl.64.4.256

Kvenild, C., & Calkins, K. (2011). *Embedded librarians: Moving beyond one-shot instruction.* Chicago, IL: Association of College and Research Libraries.

Kwon, N., & Gregory, V. L. (2012). Using transaction logs to study the effectiveness of librarian behaviors on user satisfaction in a virtual setting: A mixed-method approach. In P. Zaraté (Ed.), *Integrated and strategic advancements in decision making support systems* (pp. 120–126). Hershey, PA: IGI Global.

Lang, J. M. (2014, September 29). Stop blaming your students for your listless classroom: How the use of games as a teaching methodology has the potential to break the long history of student disengagement in college learning. *The Chronicle of Higher Education*. Retrieved from http://chronicle.com/article/Stop-Blaming-Students-for-Your/149067/

Lang, J. M. (2016, January 11). Small changes in teaching: The first 5 minutes of class. *The Chronicle of Higher Education*. Retrieved from http://chronicle.com/article/Small-Changes-in-Teaching-The/234869

Lenholt, R., Costello, B., & Stryker, J. (2003). Utilizing Blackboard to provide library instruction: Uploading MS Word handouts with links to course specific resources. *Reference Services Review, 31*(3), 211–218. doi:10.1108/00907320310486809

Lesonsky, R. (2016, August 23). Marketing to the Forgotten Generation. Retrieved from https://www.score.org/blog/marketing-forgotten-generation.

Levine, F. M., & Fasnacht, G. (1974). Token rewards may lead to token learning. *American Psychologist, 29*(11), 816–820.

Liu, Z. (1993). Difficulties and characteristics of students from developing countries in using American libraries, *College & Research Libraries,. 54*(1), 25–31. doi:10.5860/crl_54_01_25

Lynch, M. J. (n.d.). *Racial and ethnic diversity among librarians: A status report.* Retrieved from http://www.ala.org/research/librarystaffstats/diversity/racialethnic

Macfarlane, B. (2007). Beyond performance in teaching excellence. In A. Skelton (Ed.), *International perspectives on teaching excellence in higher education: Improving knowledge and practice* (pp. 48–59). New York, NY: Routledge.

Macheski, G. E., Lowney, K. S., Buhrmann, J., & Bush, M. E. L. (2008). Overcoming student disengagement and anxiety in theory, methods, and statistics courses by building a community of learners. *Teaching Sociology, 36*, 42–48. doi:10.1177/0092055X0803600106

Mader, C. E. (2009). "I Will Never Teach the Old Way Again": Classroom Management and External Incentives. *Theory Into Practice, 48*(2), 147–155.

Main, E. (2004). Student disengagement in higher education: Two trends in technology. *Journal of Educational Media & Library Sciences, 41*(3), 337–349.

Manuel, K., Beck, S. E., & Molloy, M. (2005). An ethnographic study of attitudes influencing faculty collaboration in library instruction. *The Reference Librarian, 43*(89/90), 139–161. doi:10.1300/J120v43n89_10

Marciano, P. (2011, May 13). *Motivation vs. engagement.* Retrieved January 18, 2016, from http://smartblogs.com/leadership/2011/05/13/motivations-vs-engagement/

Mardikian, J., & Kesselman, M. (1995). Beyond the desk: Enhanced reference staffing for the electronic library. *Reference Services Review, 23*(1), 21–93. doi:10.1108/eb049234

Martin, H., Jr., & Murdock, J. R. (2007). *Serving lesbian, gay, bisexual, transgender, and questioning teens: A how-to-do-it-manual for librarians.* New York, NY: Neal-Schuman.

Massey-Burzio, V. (1998). From the other side of the reference desk: A focus group study. *The Journal of Academic Librarianship, 24*(3), 208–215. doi:10.1016/S0099–1333(98)90041–6

Matthews, R., & Chatterji, S. (2011). Taming the research paper. In *2009 LOEX Conference Proceedings.* Retrieved from http://commons.emich.edu/cgi/viewcontent.cgi?article=1034&context=loexconf2009

McClennen, S. A., & Maisel, R. M. (2014). *Is satire saving our nation? Mockery and American politics.* New York, NY: Palgrave Macmillan.

McDowell, S. (2000). Library instruction for lesbian, gay, bisexual, and transgendered college students. In T. E. Jacobson & H. C. Williams (Eds.), *Teaching the new library: Reaching international, senior citizens, gay/lesbian, first-generation, at-risk, graduate and returning students, and distance learners* (pp. 71–86). New York, NY: Neal-Schuman.

McGillis, L., & Toms, E. G. (2001). Usability of the academic library web site: Implications for design. *College & Research Libraries, 62*(4), 355–367. doi:10.5860/crl.62.4.355

McGuinness, C. (2006). What faculty think: Exploring the barriers to information literacy development in undergraduate education. *The Journal of Academic Librarianship, 32*(6), 573–582.

McNaron, T. A. H. (1997). *Poisoned ivy: Lesbian and gay academics confronting homophobia.* Philadelphia, PA: Temple University.

Mech, T. F., & Brooks, C. I. (1997). Anxiety and confidence in using a library by college freshmen and seniors. *Psychological Reports, 81*(3), 929–930. doi:10.2466/pr0.1997.81.3.929

Mellon, C. A. (1986). Library anxiety: A grounded theory and its development. *College & Research Libraries, 47*(2), 160–165. doi:10.5860/crl_47_02_160

Mestre, L. S. (2012). Student preference for tutorial design: A usability study. *Reference Services Review, 40*(2), 258–276. doi:10.1108/0090732121 1228318

Mitchell, E. (2008). Place planning for libraries: The space near the heart of the college. In J. M. Hurlbert (Ed.), *Defining relevancy: Managing the new academic library* (pp. 35–52). Westport, CT: Libraries Unlimited.

Mithra, H. G. (2014). Paulo Freire's educational theory and approach: A critique. *Asia Journal of Theology, 28*(1), 96.

Moeckel, N., & Presnell, J. (1995). Recognizing, understanding, and responding: A program model of library instruction services for international students. *The Reference Librarian, 24*(51/52), 309–325. doi:10.1300/J120v24n51_29

Montanelli, D. S., & Stenstrom, P. F. (1999). *People come first: User-centered academic library service.* Chicago, IL: Association of College and Research Libraries.

Montgomery, S. E., & Miller, J. (2011). The third place: The library as collaborative and community space in a time of fiscal restraint. *College & Undergraduate Libraries, 18*(2–3), 228–238. doi:10.1080/10691316.2011.577683

Morrison, R., & Garcia, L. (2011). From embedded to integrated: Digital information literacy and new teaching models for academic librarians. In *ACRL National Conference 2011*.

Mu, C. (2007). Marketing academic library resources and information services to international students from Asia. *Reference Services Review, 35*(4), 571–583. doi:10.1108/00907320710838390

Myers, J. E., & Mobley, A. K. (2004). Wellness of undergraduates: Comparisons of traditional and nontraditional students. *Journal of College Counseling, 7*(1), 40–49. Retrieved from http://search.proquest.com/docview/213735 452?accountid=15180

National Center on Universal Design for Learning. (2014, July 31). *What is universal design for learning?* Retrieved from http://www.udlcenter.org/aboutudl/whatisudl

Natowitz, A. (1995). International students in US academic libraries: Recent concerns and trends. *Research Strategies, 13*(1), 4–16.

The New Strategist Editors. (2015). *The millennials: Americans born 1977 to 1994.* Amityville, NY: New Strategist Press.

Nichols, J., Shaffer, B., & Shockey, K. (2003). Changing the face of instruction: Is online or in-class more effective? *College & Research Libraries, 64*(5), 378–388. doi:10.5860/crl.64.5.378

Onwuegbuzie, A. J., & Jiao, Q. G. (1998). The relationship between library anxiety and learning styles among graduate students: Implications for library instruction. *Library & Information Science Research, 20*(3), 235–249. doi:10.1016/S0740–8188(98)90042–1

Onwuegbuzie, A. J., Jiao, Q. G., & Bostick, S. L. (2004). *Library anxiety: Theory, research and applications.* Lanham, MD: Scarecrow Press.

Orr, R. H. (1973). Measuring the goodness of library services: A general framework for considering quantitative measures. *Journal of Documentation, 29*(3), 315–332. doi:10.1108/eb026561

Osterman, A. C. (2008). Student response systems: Keeping the students engaged. *College & Undergraduate Libraries, 14*(4), 49–57. doi:10.1080/10691310802046801

Ouellette, D. (2011). Subject guides in academic libraries: A user-centred study of uses and perceptions/Les guides par sujets dans les bibliothèques académiques: Une étude des utilisations et des perceptions centrée sur l'utilisateur. *Canadian Journal of Information and Library Science, 35*(4), 436–451. doi:10.1353/ils.2011.0024

Parham, L. (2006). Final thoughts on diversity in libraries. In B. I. Dewey & L. Parham (Eds.), *Achieving diversity: A how-to-do-it manual for librarians* (pp. 203–204). New York, NY: Neal-Schuman.

Patton, B.A. (2002). International students and the American University Library. (ERIC Document Reproduction Service No. ED469).

Park, K. (2015). *LGBT.* Retrieved from http://libguides.com.edu/lgbt

PBS NewsHour. (2015, November 20). Hip-hop and history blend for Broadway hit "Hamilton" (Video file). Retrieved from https://youtube/HAiEVjW-GNA

Pearce, A. (2010). Text message reference at NYU libraries. *The Reference Librarian, 51*(4), 256–263.

Perry, A. (2014). The Library Minute. Arizona State University Libraries. Retrieved from https://www.youtube.com/playlist?list=PLCA6A813AA9 C9A574

Polger, M. A. (2011). Student preferences in library website vocabulary. *Library Philosophy and Practice.* Retrieved from http://digitalcommons.unl.edu/cgi/viewcontent.cgi?article=1650&context=libphilprac

Polger, M. A., & Okamoto, K. (2012). Selective (and subtle) marketing of library instruction. In C. Smallwood, V. Gubnitskaia, & K. Harrod (Eds.), *Marketing your library: Tips and tools that work* (pp. 183–190). Jefferson, NC: McFarland.

Polger, M. A., & Okamoto, K. (2014). Blending, mixing, and processing: Strategies used to engage students in the classroom. In *Proceedings of the 40th Annual LOEX Conference*, 3–5 May, 2012, Columbus, OH.

Polger, M. A., & Stempler, A. F. (2014). Out with the old, in with the new: Best practices for replacing library signage. *Public Services Quarterly, 10*(2), 67–95. doi:10.1080/15228959.2014.904210

Polkinghorne, S. (2015). *Unpacking and overcoming "edutainment" in library instruction.* Retrieved from http://www.inthelibrarywiththeleadpipe.org

Postman, N. (2006). *Amusing ourselves to death: Public discourse in the age of show business.* New York, NY: Penguin.

Prensky, M. (2009). H. sapiens digital: From digital immigrants and digital natives to digital wisdom. *Innovate: Journal of online education, 5*(3), 1.

Rader, H. B. (1980). Reference services as a teaching function. *Library Trends, 29*(1), 95–103.

Radford, M. L., & Connaway, L. S. (2013). Not dead yet! A longitudinal study of query type and ready reference accuracy in live chat and IM reference. *Library & Information Science Research, 35*(1), 2–13. doi:10.1016/j.lisr.2012.08.001

Ramsey, D. X. (2015, December 21). The missing black millennials. *The New York Times.* Retrieved from http://www.nytimes.com/2015/12/21/opinion/campaign-stops/the-missing-black-millennials.html?partner=rssnyt&emc=rss

Ratliff, A. F. (2011). Are they listening? Social media on campuses of higher education. *Journal of the Australia and New Zealand Student Services Association, 38,* 65–66. Retrieved from http://anzssa.squarespace.com/complete-editions/

Ravizza, S. M., Hambrick, D. Z., & Fenn, K. M. (2014). Non-academic internet use in the classroom is negatively related to classroom learning regardless of intellectual ability. *Computers & Education, 78,* 109–114. doi:10.1016/j.compedu.2014.05.007

Reed, M. J., Kinder, D., & Farnum, C. (2007). Collaboration between librarians and teaching faculty to teach information literacy at one Ontario university: Experiences and outcomes. *Journal of Information Literacy, 1*(3), 29–46. doi:10.11645/1.3.28

Reilly, M., & Shen, H. (2011). Shared note-taking: A smartphone-based approach to increased student engagement in lectures. In *The 11th International Workshop on Collaborative Editing Systems in Conjunction with ACM Conference on Computer Supported Cooperative Work*.

Renfro, A. (2012, December 5). *Getting smart: Meet generation Z*. Retrieved from http://gettingsmart.com/2012/12/meet-generation-z/

Renn, K. A. (1998). Lesbian, gay, bisexual, and transgender students in the college classroom. In R. L. Sanlo (Ed.), *Working with lesbian, gay, bisexual, and transgender college students: A handbook for faculty and administrators* (pp. 231–237). Westport, CT: Greenwood.

Rhoades J. G., Jr., & Hartsell, A. (2008). Marketing first impressions: Academic libraries creating partnerships and connections at new student orientations. *Library Philosophy and Practice*. Retrieved from http://digitalcommons.unl.edu/libphilprac/

Richtel, M. (2011, April 11). Multitasking takes toll on memory, study finds. *The New York Times*. Retrieved from http://bits.blogs.nytimes.com/2011/04/11/multitasking-takes-toll-on-memory-study-finds/

Riehle, C. F., & Weiner, S. A. (2013). High-impact educational practices: An exploration of the role of information literacy. *College & Undergraduate Libraries, 20*(2), 127–143. doi:10.1080/10691316.2013.789658

Robb, M., & Shellenbarger, T. (2012). Using technology to promote mobile learning: Engaging students with cell phones in the classroom. *Nurse Educator, 37*(6), 258–261. doi:10.1097/NNE.0b013e31826f27da

Rodriguez, J. E. (2016). A massively flipped class. *Reference Services Review, 44*(1), 4–20.

Rodwell, J., & Fairbairn, L. (2008). Dangerous liaisons? Defining the faculty liaison librarian service model, its effectiveness and sustainability. *Library Management, 29*(1/2), 116–124. doi:10.1108/01435120810844694

Romal, J. B. (2008). Use of humor as a pedagogical tool for accounting education. *Academy of Educational Leadership Journal, 12*(1), 83–106. Retrieved from http://www.alliedacademies.org/Public/AffiliateAcademies/ael.aspx

Roy, L., & Hensley, M. K. (2016). Helping LIS students understand the reference librarian's teacher identity. *The Reference Librarian, 57*(4), 336–340. doi:10.1080/02763877.2016.1146562

Rumble, J., & Noe, N. (2009). Project SAILS: Launching information literacy assessment across university waters. *Technical Services Quarterly, 26*(4), 287–298. doi:10.1080/07317130802678936

Saeed, S., & Zyngier, D. (2012). How motivation influences student engagement: A qualitative case study. *Journal of Education and Learning, 1*(2), 252–267.

Sana, F., Weston, T., & Cepeda, N.J. (2013). Laptop multitasking hinders classroom learning for both users and nearby peers. *Computers & Education, 62,* 24–31. doi:10.1016/j.compedu.2012.10.003

Sanborn, L. (2005). Perspectives on . . . improving library instruction: Faculty collaboration. *The Journal of Academic Librarianship, 31*(5), 477–481. doi:10.1016/j.acalib.2005.05.010

Sandy, J. H., Krishnamurthy, M., & Rau, W. (2009). An innovative approach for creating a self-guided video tour in an academic library. *The Southeastern Librarian, 57*(3), 5.

Schulten, K., Gross, S., & Gonchar, M. (2016, March 24). The ten-dollar founding father without a father: teaching and learning with "Hamilton." [Web log comment]. Retrieved from http://learning.blogs.nytimes.com/2016/03/24/the-ten-dollar-founding-father-without-a-father-teaching-and-learning-with-hamilton/ ?_r=1

Scull, A. (2014). Fostering student engagement and collaboration with the library: Student creation of LibGuides as a research assignment. *The Reference Librarian, 55*(4), 318–327. doi:10.1080/02763877.2014.929076

Seamans, N. H. (2002). Student perceptions of information literacy: Insights for librarians. *Reference Services Review, 30*(2), 112–123. doi:10.1108/00907320210428679

Seeholzer, J., & Salem, J. A. (2011). Library on the go: A focus group study of the mobile web and the academic library. *College & Research Libraries, 72*(1), 9–20. doi:10.5860/crl-65r1

Sen, B. (2006). Defining market orientation for libraries. *Library Management, 27*(4/5), 201–217.

Sheidlower, S. (2008, January). *Teaching disabled students: Emphasis on their abilities, not their disabilities.* Paper presented at the midwinter meeting of the American Library Association; the Association of College & Research Libraries' Instruction Section current issue discussion, Philadelphia, PA.

Sherbill, A. (2015, January). 4 new "effective teaching" methods to WOW your students. [Web blog post]. Retrieved from http://www.powtoon.com/blog/effective-teaching/

Silver, S. L., & Nickel, L. T. (2005). Are online tutorials effective? A comparison of online and classroom library instruction methods. *Research Strategies, 20*(4), 389–396. doi:10.1016/j.resstr.2006.12.012

Skinner, E. A., & Belmont, M. J. (1993). Motivation in the classroom: Reciprocal effects of teacher behavior and student engagement across the school year. *Journal of educational Psychology, 85*(4), 571. doi:10.1037/0022–0663.85.4.571

Smallwood, C. (Ed.). (2012). *Library services for multicultural patrons: Strategies to encourage library use.* New York, NY: Scarecrow Press.

Smith, A. L., & Baker, L. (2011). Getting a clue: Creating student detectives and dragon slayers in your library. *Reference Services Review, 39*(4), 628–642. doi:10.1108/00907321111186659

Smith, L., & Rivera, E. (2004, February 2). Turning librarians into babysitters; on snow days, parents leaving children unattended at Fairfax facilities. *Washington Post*. Retrieved from https://www.washingtonpost.com

Smith, S. D., & Galbraith, Q. (2011). Shopping carts and student employees: How student committees can bring innovative ideas to academic libraries. *College & Research Libraries News, 72*(7), 394–397.

Snavely, L. (2012). Engaging undergraduates with the academic library. In L. Snavely (Ed.), *Student engagement and the academic library* (pp. 1–10). Santa Barbara, CA: Libraries Unlimited.

Sosteric, M., & Hesemeier, S. (2002). When is a learning object not an object: A first step towards a theory of learning objects. *The International Review of Research in Open and Distributed Learning, 3*(2). Retrieved from http://www.irrodl.org/index.php/irrodl/article/view/106/185

Stansberry, K. (n.d.). Understanding individualized education programs. *Understood for learning and attention issues: School and learning.* Retrieved from https://www.understood.org/en/school-learning/special-services/ieps/understanding-individualized-education-programs

Stebbins, L. F. (2015). *Finding reliable information online: Adventures of an information sleuth.* Lanham, MD: Rowman & Littlefield.

Stein, L. L., & Lamb, J. M. (1998). Not just another BI: Faculty-librarian collaboration to guide students through the research process. *Research Strategies, 16*(1), 29–39. doi:10.1016/S0734-3310(98)90004-0

Stevens, R. H. (2010). Managing human capital: How to use knowledge management to transfer knowledge in today's multi-generational workforce. *International Business Research, 3*(3), 77–83. Retrieved from http://search.proquest.com/docview/822240347?accountid=15180

Stone, V. L., Bongiorno, R., Hinegardner, P. G., & Williams, M. A. (2004). Delivery of web-based instruction using Blackboard: A collaborative project. *Journal of the Medical Library Association, 92*(3), 375.

Stonebraker, I. (2015). Flipping the business information literacy classroom: Redesign, implementation, and assessment of a case study. *Journal of Business & Finance Librarianship, 20*(4), 283–301. doi:10.1080/08963568.2015.1072893

Strayer, J. F. (2012). How learning in an inverted classroom influences cooperation, innovation and task orientation. *Learning Environments Research, 15*(2), 171–193. doi:10.1007/s10984-012-9108-4

Tapscott, D. (2009). *Grown up digital: How the net generation is changing the world.* New York, NY: McGraw Hill.

Targum, S. D., & Rosenthal, N. (2008). "Seasonal affective disorder." *Psychiatry (Edgemont), 5*(5), 31–33. Retrieved from http://www.ncbi.nlm.nih.gov/pmc/articles/PMC2686645/

Tatum, B. D. (1997). *"Why are all the Black kids sitting together in the cafeteria?": And other conversations about race.* New York, NY: Basic.

Taylor, P. (2014). *The next America: Boomers, millennials, and the looming generational showdown.* New York, NY: Public Affairs.

Tempelman-Kluit, N., & Ehrenberg, E. (2003). Library instruction and online tutorials: Developing best practices for streaming desktop video capture. *Feliciter, 49*(2), 89–90.

Thaler, M. (2008). *The librarian from the black lagoon.* New York, NY: Cartwheel Books.

Thompson, R. (2016, June 6). *Explaining Boolean without Venn diagrams.* [Electronic mailing list message]. Retrieved from http://lists.ala.org/sympa/info/ili-l

Tobias, C., & Blair, A. (2015). Listen to what you cannot hear, observe what you cannot see: An introduction to evidence-based methods for evaluating and enhancing the user experience in distance library services. *Journal of Library & Information Services in Distance Learning, 9*(1/2), 148–156.

Torok, S. E., McMorris, R. F., & Lin, W. (2004). Is humor an appreciated teaching tool?: Perceptions of professors' teaching styles and use of humor. *College Teaching, 52*(1), 14–20. Retrieved from http://www.tandf.co.uk/journals/titles/87567555.asp

Turkle, S. (2015a, October 2). How to teach in an age of distraction. *The Chronicle of Higher Education.* Retrieved from http://chronicle.com/article/How-to-Teach-in-an-Age-of/233515

Turkle, S. (2015b, September 26). Stop googling, let's talk. *The New York Times.* Retrieved from www.nytimes.com/2015/09/27/opinion/sunday/stop-googling-lets-talk.html

Tyckoson, D. A. (2001). What is the best model of reference service? *Library Trends, 50*(2), 183–96.

University of North Carolina at Charlotte, Center for Teaching and Learning, Department of Academic Affairs. (2016). *Writing objectives using Bloom's taxonomy.* Retrieved from http://teaching.uncc.edu/learning-resources/articles-books/best-practice/goals-objectives/writing-objectives

U.S. Department of Justice, Civil Rights Division, Disability Rights Section. (n.d.). *Information and technical assistance on the Americans with Disabilities Act: Introduction to the ADA.* Retrieved from http://www.ada.gov/ada_intro.htm

VanDuinkerken, W., & Mosley, P. A. (2011). *The challenge of library management: Leading with emotional engagement.* Chicago, IL: American Library Association.

Vardeman, K. K., & Barba, I. (2014). Reference in 160 characters or less: The role of text messaging in virtual reference services. *Internet Reference Services Quarterly, 19*(3/4), 163–179.

Vecchione, A., & Ruppel, M. (2012). Reference is neither here nor there: A snapshot of SMS reference services. *The Reference Librarian, 53*(4), 355–372. doi:10.1080/02763877.2012.704569

Venter, P., Wright, A., & Dibb, S. (2015). Performing market segmentation: A performative perspective. *Journal of Marketing Management, 31*(1–2), 62–83.

Viggiano, R., & Ault, M. (2001). Online library instruction for online students. *Information Technology and Libraries, 20*(3), 135.

Vossler, J., & Sheidlower, S. (2011). *Humor and information literacy: Practical techniques for library instruction*. Santa Barbara, CA: Libraries Unlimited.

Vossler, J., & Watts, J. (2011, May). *Intentional edutainment: A pedagogically and theatrically sound approach to information literacy instruction*. In the thirty-ninth annual Library Orientation Exchange [LOEX] conference, Fort Worth, TX. Retrieved from http://www.loexconference.org/2011/program/sessions.html

Walker, B. E. (2008). This is jeopardy! An exciting approach to learning in library instruction. *Reference Services Review, 36*(4), 381–388. doi:10.1108/00907320810920351

Wallace, L. K. (2004). *Libraries, mission & marketing: Writing mission statements that work*. Chicago, IL: American Library Association.

Walsh, A. (2009). Text messaging (SMS) and libraries. *Library Hi Tech News, 26*(8), 9–11.

Ward, J., Mervar, D., Loving, M., & Kronen, S. (2013). Can a small/medium-sized library manage live online reference? In Bill Katz (Ed.), *Digital reference services* (pp. 311–322). New York, NY: Routledge.

Washor, E., & Mojkowski, C. (2014). Student disengagement: It's deeper than you think. *Student Learning: Engagement and Motivation, 95*(8), 8–10.

Waugh, J. (2013). Formality in chat reference: Perceptions of 17- to 25-year-old university students. *Evidence Based Library and Information Practice, 8*(1), 19–34. doi:10.18438/B8WS48

Webb, K. K., & Hoover, J. (2015). Universal design for learning (UDL) in the academic library: A methodology for mapping multiple means of representation in library tutorials. *College & Research Libraries, 76*(4), 537–553, 10.5860/crl.76.4.537

Webb, K. M., Schaller, M. A., & Hunley, S. A. (2008). Measuring library space use and preferences: Charting a path toward increased engagement. *Portal: Libraries and the Academy, 8*(4), 407–422.

Westwood, P. (2009). *What teachers need to know about students with disabilities*. Victoria, AU: ACER Press.

White, G. W. (2012). Developing a marketing plan for the library by and for students. In L. Snavely (Ed.), *Student engagement and the academic library* (pp. 1–10). Santa Barbara, CA: Libraries Unlimited.

Wiatco Internet Services. (n.d.). WorkJoke: Funny physicists jokes. Retrieved July 27, 2015, from http://www.workjoke.com/physicists-jokes.html

Wiedmer, T. T. (2015). Generations do differ: Best practices in leading traditionalists, boomers, and generations X, Y, and Z. *Delta Kappa Gamma Bulletin, 82*(1), 51–58.

Wilcox Brooks, A. (2014). Information literacy and the flipped classroom. *Communications in Information Literacy, 8*(2), 225–235.

Wilson, J. M. (2000). Group identity and social trust in the American public. In *Annual meeting of the American Political Science Association*, Washington, DC, August.

Wilson, L. A. (1995). Building the user-centered library. *RQ, 34*(3), 297–303.

Wilson, P. (1979). Librarians as teachers: The study of an organization fiction. *The Library Quarterly, 49*(2), 146–162.

Wolfe, L. A. (2005). *Library public relations, promotions, and communications.* Chicago, IL: Neal-Schuman.

Woodard, B. S. (2005). One-on-one instruction: From the reference desk to online chat. *Reference & User Services Quarterly, 44*(3), 203–209.

Wyles, B. A. (1998). Adjunct faculty in the community college: Realities and challenges. *New Directions for Higher Education, 1998*(104), 89–93. doi:10.1002/he.10409

Xiao, J. (2010). Integrating information literacy into Blackboard: Librarian-faculty collaboration for successful student learning. *Library Management, 31*(8/9), 654–668. doi:10.1108/01435121011093423

Yang, S. (2009). Information literacy online tutorials: An introduction to rationale and technological tools in tutorial creation. *The Electronic Library, 27*(4), 684–693. doi:10.1108/02640470910979624

Yi, H. (2005). Library instruction goes online: An inevitable trend. *Library Review, 54*(1), 47–58. doi:10.1108/00242530510574156

Yi, Z., Lodge, D., & McCausland, S. (2013). Australian academic librarians' perceptions of marketing services and resources. *Library Management, 34*(8/9), 585–602.

York, A. C., & Vance, J. M. (2009). Taking library instruction into the online classroom: Best practices for embedded librarians. *Journal of Library Administration, 49*(1/2), 197–209. doi:10.1080/01930820802312995

Yosso, T., Smith, W., Ceja, M., & Solórzano, D. (2009). Critical race theory, racial microaggressions, and campus racial climate for Latina/o undergraduates. *Harvard Educational Review, 79*(4), 659–691. doi:10.17763/haer.79.4.m6867014157m7071

Young, N. J., & Von Seggern, M. (2001). General information seeking in changing times: A focus group study. *Reference & User Services Quarterly, 41*(2), 159–169.

Zhao, C. M., & Kuh, G. D. (2004). Adding value: Learning communities and student engagement. *Research in Higher Education, 45*(2), 115–138. doi:10.1023/B:RIHE.0000015692.88534.de

Zhong, Y. (2012). Universal design for learning (UDL) in library instruction. *College & Undergraduate Libraries, 19*(1), 33–45. doi:10.1080/10691316.2012.652549

Ziv, A. (1976). Facilitating effects of humor on creativity. *Journal of Educational Psychology. 68*(3), 318–322. Retrieved from http://www.apa.org/pubs/journals/edu/index.aspx

Index

About the Authors

Mark Aaron Polger is assistant professor and first year experience librarian at the College of Staten Island, City University of New York. He is also an adjunct Information Literacy instructor at ASA College in Midtown Manhattan. He has published and presented in the areas of library marketing, user experience research, and instructional practices. He is most interested in how users experience the library and its services through various promotional strategies. He is originally from Montreal, Canada, and moved to New York City in 2008.

Scott Sheidlower is associate professor and head of circulation, reserves, and archivist at York College, City University of New York. He has published several biographical articles relating to various topics from terrorism to American cinema. He is the coauthor (with Joshua Vossler) of *Humor and Information Literacy: Practical Techniques for Library Instruction*. Sheidlower has presented at several conferences as both an invited keynote speaker and a panelist on topics ranging from humor and teaching in the library to working with the disabled in library settings.